Collecting Old Toy Soldiers

Collecting Old Toy Soldiers

Ian McKenzie

photography by Michael Hallett

B. T. Batsford Ltd,
London & Sydney

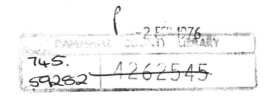
First published 1975
© Ian McKenzie 1975
ISBN 0 7134 3036 2

Filmset by Servis Filmsetting Ltd, Manchester

Printed and bound in Great Britain by
Butler & Tanner Ltd, Frome
for the publishers B.T.Batsford Ltd,
4 Fitzhardinge Street, London W1H 0AH
& 23 Cross Street, Brookvale, NSW, 2100
Australia

TO MY MOTHER AND FATHER

Contents

Acknowledgements

I would like to record my gratitude to the many people who have assisted me in the compilation and production of this book. Without their help, kindness and advice, so freely given, it would never have materialised.

To my friends: Alan Grieve who 'introduced' me to toy soldiers and allowed me the freedom of his collection for photographic purposes. Patrick Murray MBE, founder and formerly curator of the Museum of Childhood Edinburgh, for his Foreword, historical information, use of his library and toy collection and checking the manuscript. Michael Hallett, Principal Lecturer at Birmingham Polytechnic, for putting up with incredible privations in all parts of the country, and then producing such excellent photographs. Ahmed Youssef, Senior Conservation Officer of the North West Museums and Art Galleries Service, for writing the section on conservation and restoration. John Hinnells, Lecturer at Manchester University for encouraging me to write the book, and Robin Malcolm for his help with the manuscript.

I also wish to express my thanks to Jock Coutts of 'Under Two Flags' for the use of his collection and his shop for photography in London; His Grace the Duke of Marlborough who permitted the photographing of his collection, and Mr P Duffie of the Blenheim Estate whose coffee and understanding made the work such a pleasure; Mr M I McGregor whose zeal in chasing manufacturers helped in obtaining specimens for photography; Mr J Murphy of the Department of Polymer Technology at Manchester Polytechnic for identifying types of plastic; Phillip Reading for the use of pieces from his collection; Tony Ross, Senior Lecturer at Manchester Polytechnic for the use of pieces from his collection, and Ken Bowers for advice on publishing.

Kind assistance was also offered by J Wilhelm, Musée Carnavalet, Paris; Colonel Martel, Musée de l'Armée, Paris; Caroline Goodfellow, Bethnal Green Museum, London; Victoria Trollope, the London Museum, Kensington Palace; Mrs J D Fudge, Luton Museums Division; Bridget Yates and David Young, Stranger's Hall Museum, Nor-

9

wich; Marion Waller and Yootha Rose, Rottingdean Grange & National Toy Museum; Mrs C Whitehead, Sudbury Hall, Derby; R G E Sandbach, Tunbridge Wells Museum, Kent; J G Kerkhoven, Leyden Museum, Holland; E Heer, Grandson Castle Museum, Switzerland; Agathe Müller, Kunstmuseum Lucerne, Switzerland; J D Kilbourne, Anderson House Museum, Washington DC, USA; J Noble, Museum of the City of New York, USA; A Duchesne, Musée Royal de l'Armée, Brussels; Dr W Baer, Verwaltung der Staatlichen Schlösser und Garten, Berlin; Dr Leister, Bomann Museum, Celle; Dr P Jaeckel, Bayer Armeemuseum; Rear Admiral Streubel, Armeemuseum der Deutschen Demokratischen Republik, Dresden; I A Hoefer, Kestner Museum, Hanover; Dr Zankl, Historisches Museum, Hanover; H Stöblein, Deutches Zinnfigurenmuseum, Kulmback-Plassenburg; Heide Thiel, Kaiser Wilhelm Museum, Krefeld; Dr L Wenzel, Museum für Geschichte der Stadt, Leipzig; Dr Leonie von Wilckens, Germanisches Nationalmuseum, Nurnberg; Dr R Wendt, Historisches Museum, Schwerin; H Gaub, Deutsches Spielzeugmuseum, Thuringen.

The curators of the following museums: Östereichisches Zinnfigurenmuseum, Vienna; Musée de Cluny, Paris; Pollock's Toy Museum, London; Biberach Museum; Stadtmuseum, Weimar; Städtisches Museum, Zwickau; Swiss National Museum, Zurich.

Finally I would like to thank, on behalf of Michael Hallett and myself, Mr & Mrs A M Grieve, Mrs M Hallett, Mr & Mrs K A S Leslie, Mr & Mrs R S W Malcolm and Mr & Mrs J A McKenzie for their hospitality; my wife for her understanding and patience while material was being translated, written, photographed and typed; and Jamie (aged two) for reducing his demands on my time.

Foreword

Few hobbies in Britain have had such an astonishing success as that of the miniature soldier. Supreme now, 50 years ago there were not 20 collectors of militaria in the country and the little figure was not well known. There was no book on the subject in English and the only one at all was the German 'Der Zinnsoldat', by Theodor Hampe, published in Berlin in 1924. Significantly its subtitle was 'Ein Deutsches Spielzug' – a German Toy.

Mr McKenzie's book is about the toy soldier and he tackles the subject vigorously and from an entirely adult viewpoint. From the collector's angle therefore, the book is extremely valuable. Not only for the collector of the figure as a toy, but also from the point of view of the more elaborate uniform or period piece. The book is a mine of all sorts of information dealing with the figures of all nations and also with their cleaning, repairing and storage. His warnings about the risks attendant on improper storage are most grisly reading.

He even steers for us an undeviating course through the jungle of William Britain's figures and has much of interest to say about those of his rivals and pirates. For this part alone we should be grateful.

He also deals with other figure types including that shamefully neglected branch the paper, cut-out figure. Nor does he forget to mention the wooden soldier of the Victorian nursery tale; something of a collector's piece today with his trim figure, staring beady eyes and monstrous head gear.

It is a truism that a book of this nature, published at the right time, often proves to be a turning point in any given culture. One would like to think that the toy soldier will henceforth take his rightful place in the ranks beside his younger brother, the model.

Patrick Murray MBE FSA
Edinburgh

Author's Note

The terminology used to describe basic categories of toy soldiers in this book may be briefly described as follows: 'Flats' are a maximum of 1mm thick, the figure is created on a single plane and can only be viewed from the back or front. 'Semi-solids' indicates a thicker figure, but not fully three dimensional. 'Solids' are fully three dimensional, capable of being viewed from any angle and the casting is filled with metal. 'Hollow-cast' refers to fully three dimensional figures consisting only of a metal skin, hollow inside. These terms and their implications are explained more fully in the text.

The traditional method of measuring a figure is from the base to the top of the bare head of a man at attention. This lacks precision for the purpose of this book. To be more accurate figures in plates have been measured from the base to the top of the hat not including any plumes.

1 Introduction

Figure 1
Flat metal soldier. Roman
*c.*250 AD 60mm.

Figure 2
Flat metal pilgrim's token
depicting St Thomas à
Becket. Late 13th or 14th
century.

Figure 3
Flat metal knight, possibly
St Denis. French 14th
century. 60mm.

Historical Background

It is in the nature of man to be warlike both as a hunter of animals
and as a killer of his own species. He invents weapons to help in these
pursuits and wears finery to differentiate himself from those who are
not warriors. It is also in his nature to paint likenesses and make
models of his everyday life.

This production of miniature hunters and soldiers is recorded with
certainty for about 2500 years, in fact from the period of the Middle
Kingdom in Egypt. The best known examples are groups of painted
wooden infantry figures commonly found in the tombs of Pharaohs
and high-ranking princes. The mediterranean islands provide another
source of tiny warriors from about 800 BC, and from Classical Greece
came bronze, clay and wooden soldiers. The Romans made flat metal
figurines of gods, goddesses, soldiers (Fig 1), gladiators and personalities, many engraved on one side only. A great number of these early
pieces from Egypt, Italy, Greece, Spain and China were votive
offerings, grave furnishings or household statuettes, and not made to
be played with. There is however doubt in some cases. Where jointed
dolls and terracotta or bronze warriors have been found together in a
child's grave the warriors may have been toys taken from this world
to be played with in the next.

The Middle Ages was a period of intense aggressive rivalry in
Europe with many local and national issues at stake. Much of the
sport and physical activity was geared towards military prowess, so
quite naturally a boy's playthings, apart from weapons, were
miniature knights on foot and horseback. In the twelfth century hand-
manipulated toy knights were played with. From that date on large
numbers of metal and pottery figures were made many of which are
still in existance.

Many of these metal figures are pilgrim's tokens or charms depicting the better-known saints (Fig 2). They would be carried or worn
either as mementos of a visit or in the hope of ensuring safe passage
through a war. Some are simple and beautifully designed with little
quatrefoil stands, reminiscent of German flat toy soldiers of the
mid-eighteenth century (Fig 3).

The more obvious jousting toys are jointed dolls in full armour, mounted on cloth-caparisoned wooden horses. They are perfectly detailed, expertly made and run on wheeled wooden bases. These and later hand-made figures in gold, silver or pewter could only be afforded by the very wealthy. Kings and princes had whole armies made from these precious metals. Louis XIII had 300 silver soldiers and Napoleon's son, the King of Rome, had 117 soldiers made of gold. Also during that period ingenious automata were made using complex mechanisms to march, fire, countermarch and perform drill sequences. With such toys potential rulers play-learned the rudiments of military manoeuvre. Instructive games of a martial nature were very necessary as the princes might at any time be faced with the command of a real army in the field.

Unfortunately most of these and other precious historical figures have disappeared. Probably melted down to pay the wages of real troops or broken up in times of idealogical stress.

Soldiers for Pleasure

Toy soldiers had been carved in wood and cut from paper sheets for some considerable time when mass produced tin figures first appeared at the beginning of the eighteenth century in Europe. The introduction of low-priced pieces transformed collecting and playing with toy soldiers into a pleasure shared by almost every boy, young and not so young, all over the world.

These figures and their descendants have occasioned many happy memories of childhood; of cherished regiments being set out on the dining-room table in battle formation; of armies moving into action with well tried heroes to the front, chipped and broken as reminders of their former glory; of red-coated guardsmen tenaciously defending a corner of the garden until the last matchstick-mended figure was killed at his post. Just as seriously, though with perhaps more lasting effect, figures were used by military establishments to enact complex ceremonial duties or to demonstrate tactics for the benefit of real-life participants.

Handling these tiny fighting men with their shiny paint and movable arms has always been a great delight. They were special toys from the moment the manufacturer's box was opened to reveal them. Hans Anderson's tale of 'The Constant Tin Soldier' sums up these feelings in the opening paragraph:

> There were five and twenty tin soldiers, all brothers, for they had all been made out of the same old tin spoon. They carried muskets and held themselves very upright, and their uniforms were red and blue, very gay indeed. The first word they heard in this world, when the lid was taken off the box was 'Tin Soldiers!' It

was a little boy who had made this exclamation, clapping his hands at the same time. They had been given to him because it was his birthday, and he now set them out on the table.

Toy soldiers were made to be played with; to give pleasure in creating situations of martial fantasy or to re-enact historic and contemporary battles. It was H G Wells, an ardent war-gamer, who formulated and had published in 1913 a set of rules entitled *Little Wars*. This served to make the hobby more popular and encouraged 'owner-generals' to gather larger and more diverse forces.

A child's toys are his means of coming to terms with the adult world and generally they reflect accurately the society which made them. Through his toys the child learns about people, human relationships, organisation, co-ordination and many of the other basic skills of living. But when he grows out of a toy it is generally discarded without a second thought. Toy soldiers suffer this fate along with a mixture of dolls, balls and games. Lucky are the soldiers, however battle scarred, that are packed away for another generation of little generals to play with. Many of them, thanks to careful parents, have survived to become the much sought after collectors pieces of today.

Collections, Collectors & Antiques
There are numerous collections of toy soldiers both in private hands and in museums. As one might expect the largest number of collections is housed in museums in Germany where the mass-produced toy soldier was born. France, too, has its share of large and interesting collections. Britain cannot boast any major museum collections and unfortunately very few minor ones.

All collections vary in purpose and content, this often shows as a local or national characteristic. In Germany for instance, there is a tendency towards flats in diorama form depicting historic, social and mythical events. At the opposite end of the scale a regimental museum may concentrate wholly on the uniform of its founding regiment. Most of the best collections in Britain, Europe and the United States of America are in private hands, and consequently are only available to a limited number of people.

Toys which have been played with, cared for and handed down from one generation to the next carry with them an inexplicable aura of the past. As production has declined, and in some countries ceased, their rarity has attracted an increasing number of collectors. Many figures are over 200 years old, and as antiques have a rapidly rising financial value. No longer shot at with dried peas and matchsticks from spring-operated cannon, but kept in as perfect condition as possible they are displayed for their antique, aesthetic and nostalgic qualities, and as important items of social history in a scantily documented area.

The recent boom in popularity of general militaria has resulted in dealers setting up shop to specialise in these types of goods. So that toy soldiers mingle on shelves with model soldiers. It will be useful at this point to define the very distinct differences between them.

Toy soldiers are, as the name implies, playthings made (ostensibly at least) for the pleasure of children. They generally march through life in rather elegant and formal postures, covered in shiny paint. The necessity of painting large quantities means that the uniform is quite basic and shows scant detail. There are four main varieties, flats, semi-solids, solids and hollow-casts coming in sizes from 20mm upwards.

Model soldiers, which had their beginnings between the two world wars, are an attempt to create in miniature an exact replica of a man in military uniform. The uniform should be correct in every detail, and the figure's posture animated to appear as life-like as possible. Being on the whole more expensive and more carefully painted than their toy counterparts, they were conceived not as playthings but as statuettes. Mostly solid and three dimensional they are made in a variety of sizes from 30mm upwards.

Most serious collectors want to know as much as possible about their subject, delving deeply into its many and varied facets. The acquisition of information apart from being a most fascinating and rewarding aspect of collecting, gives substance and a greater degree of appreciation to the items collected. Books, catalogues, journals and dealer's lists are among the main sources of reference, along with numerous small articles in newspaper and magazines. However it is the toy soldiers themselves that are the focal point, and real knowledge can only come from seeing, handling, comparing and discussing them.

It is impossible to write an absolutely sequential history of the development of toy soldiers. The lack of early documentary evidence, catalogues or manufacturer's lists plus the considerable amount of figure piracy and simultaneous production in different countries are the main difficulties. There is however sufficient extant information to build an accurate outline making continued research all the more worth while.

This book is concerned with commercially produced toy soldiers and looks at their background, the people who made them and what they made, and compares the sizes and styles over the last two centuries. It also provides a basis of knowledge and advice on how to build a collection of your own, and where to see the principal public collections.

2 The Flat Toy Soldier

1 A slate mould used for the production of flats. The fine engraving on the figure and the air channels can be clearly seen.

Military Influences

Before discussing the commercial production of toy soldiers, it will be useful to look at the military background which strongly influenced what was to become a thriving branch of the toy industry.

Europe in the seventeenth century was a massive complex of small states and territories, most of them independently administered but holding together in various groups and confederations. There was constant bickering and rivalry between these states as they vied with each other for economic and martial precedence. This caused the enlargement of armies at an alarming rate, and having been brought into being they were then kept as permanent forces to garrison towns and patrol borders.

Armies must be supplied with clothing, food, armaments and transport. So economic and industrial structures quickly expanded to correspond with military growth. There was a general militaristic awareness developing in the minds of the people, a combination of power and pride which was to help provide the impetus for an almost continuous series of wars during the next 200 years. The main protagonists in these wars were the Kingdoms of Spain, France,

19

Hungary, Poland, Sweden, Great Britain, the Holy Roman Empire (Austria) and Russia.

During the period 1600–1800 some 18 wars were waged involving some of the best-known battles and soldiers in world history.

Frederick II (the Great) King of Prussia was the most exceptional soldier of the age, who between succeeding to the throne in 1740 and the start of the Seven Years War in 1756 already had a formidable list of military achievements to his credit. He simultaneously took on the might of Russia, Sweden, France, Saxony, Austria and other German States. Always heavily outnumbered his offensive tactics paid off and despite some setbacks he achieved remarkable victories such as Rossbach and Leuthen in 1757.

Frederick and his armies represent a very important point in the attempt to develop a sequence of toy soldiers, as they are the subjects of some of the earliest commercially produced toy soldiers by a known maker.

Two other important points have a strong bearing on the overall military picture and on the toy soldiers which derive from it. Firstly during the period 1600–1800 military clothing began to evolve into standard garments or uniforms for each section of the army. This gave a cohesive look to regiments and allowed them to be easily identified. Secondly, military training, especially under Frederick the Great, became more rigid in its conception and operation creating greater discipline and mobility.

This therefore was the background which influenced the early types of toy soldiers. Enlarged armies, martial pride, constant battles, famous soldiers, identifiable uniforms and rigidly organised bodies of troops.

The Printed Paper Soldier

There is no date for the point in time when engravings and wood-block prints, normally used to illustrate books or as decorative information and memento sheets, became cut-out toys. Until the latter half of the eighteenth century it is often difficult to differentiate between them. Their stylistic similarity follows quite naturally when the same artists were commissioned to carry out almost identical tasks. Contrary to their intended use many of these prints, from the earliest point of production, were probably cut out and pasted on to card or wood as children's playthings.

It can be reasonably assumed that printers from about 1500 onwards produced sheets of military figures which have not survived the ravages of small children or the passage of time. Certainly by the end of the seventeenth century J Steudner of Augsburg was publishing coloured sheets for an already avid market. There was a wide selection of mainly civilian subjects embracing religion, mythology, hunting, theatre and a very few military ones. In the early eighteenth century Nurnberg and Leipzig boasted healthy industries printing illustrated sheets, some of the most attractive coming from a Frenchman, Jean-Michael Papillon from 1730 onwards.

The town of Strasbourg in Alsace was a centre of high-quality printing, it also had strong military connections. When Louis xv entered the town in 1744, the pomp and pageantry of the setting prompted a printer named Seyfried to publish a set of coloured sheets representing Louis' troops.

In 1786 Jean Frederick Striedbeck set up a factory manufacturing painted soldiers, his reputation was high, his work executed with care and great attention to detail. But the pinnacle of quality was reached by Benjamin Zix around 1798, his gouache painted figures were beautifully observed and showed incredible individuality.

By the late eighteenth century paper was fast becoming a popular toy-making medium. It was relatively inexpensive compared to wood and metal, could be beautifully coloured, and allowed children to participate in the preparation of their own toys. In America dressing dolls, often personalities in children's stories, were popular while in Germany beautifully engraved cut-out peep shows and dolls' house furniture were to be bought. Commercial success brought a rash of manufacturers into the field, quality varied from the most exquisite coloured engravings to the dull and unimaginative. Most sheets were obtainable either fully coloured, or less expensively in a single black printing.

One of the great milestones in the production of cheap print came about 1798 when lithography was invented. Alois Senefelder a Munich-based Czecheslovakian is credited with its invention, but it is interesting to note that it was simultaneously being developed in France and Italy. Now larger quantities of paper soldiers could be printed in lots of varied postures, and they could be cheaply coloured. This invention coincided with one of the most publicised periods of military contention and fashion, beginning with the French Revolution and continuing through the First and Second Empires.

Numerous sheets of Napoleon's troops, portraits of marshals and famous commanders, camp scenes, guns and waggons appeared on the market. Outstanding amongst the early lithographed sheets were those produced by J G Pfluger, L Havard and R Nicker. The best known and certainly the most attractive sheets of the Second Empire were Rudolf Silbermann's. He found a method of colour printing in an oil-based ink about 1845 and was turning out some 130,000 sheets per year. Another company run by the brothers Pellerin was operating at Epinal in the Vosges. They specialised in the production of hand-coloured wood cuts, and are still in operation today although the printing process has changed.

2 Embossed paper hussar. British c.1920. 80mm.

Between the high quality output of Silbermann and the First World War, Gustave Fischbach and Fritz Kieffer at l'Imprimerie Alsacienne were the most noted exponents. It was also during this period that other military toys and card cut-outs came into prominence. Wooden building blocks of an 'instructional' nature covered in printed paper with the letters of the alphabet related to soldiers and battles; groups of soldiers, also paper-covered blocks to be set up in parade fashion with detailed instructions on their arrangement; and simple turned wood skittles.

The juvenile theatre was still in vogue as were dressing dolls. The first military dressing doll associated with a story was the *Adventures of Little Harry* which was published in England. Prick-out cigarette cards were issued by the tobacco firm of Carreras and another set were sold with Prize Crop about 1932. There was a craze for paper scraps, and their manufacturers managed to produce some lovely specimens in pre-First World War dress uniforms. Some were embossed to give a relief effect (Plate 2), others could be hinged together in lines and stood up. The coronations of Edward VII and George V were highly popular events, and elaborate cut-out coronation processions, including representatives of British and Commonwealth troops were sold.

The beautiful transparent colours, made from natural pigments, obtained by lithographers in the early 1900s are no longer seen. The assured figure drawing of illustrators like Gordon Browne and Stanley L Woode has disappeared. Modern military illustration in Britain is on the whole extremely bad and so recent excursions into paper toy soldiers tend to be of poor quality. In the main paper toys are a European phenomenon and although there have been surges of interest outside these regions from time to time, they have never maintained a strong following (Colour Plate I).

Flat Tin Soldiers

By the end of the seventeenth century there was already a strong tradition in Germany of metal figurines and charms. Mostly following a variety of the more celebrated religious and social themes. They were popular, not very expensive, and must have been selling consistently in sufficiently large numbers to have established this permanence. In their search for new and equally profitable lines the manufacturers of these trinkets did not have far to look. The prevailing military situation in Europe, as we have seen, gave them ample subject matter and was ripe for miniaturisation and commercial exploitation. It required very little extra effort to produce soldiers in place of saints,

and the general public must have shown a considerable and knowledgable interest in this new venture.

The city of Nurnberg in Southern Germany having the advantage of nearby mineral mines was the centre of this thriving industry, and handled the bulk of national production. It therefore followed quite naturally that the majority of early flat toy soldiers were also made there, starting as an experimental side line and eventually taking over the greater part of the market.

There appears to have been a number of flats produced in Italy at about the same date. Not however on the same scale or with the same success as in Germany. There are very few of these early Italian pieces still in existance, and in common with many other early toys the makers are unknown.

Examples of early German toy soldiers dating from about 1730 are rudimentary in their design and execution. Their engravers appear to have lacked all but the most elementary knowledge of human anatomy. They produced pieces usually ill-proportioned, clumsy and sometimes without such basic elements as feet (Fig 4). Yet their well-detailed uniforms present an interesting and complete contrast. Information has been obtained either by the observation of real troops or printed book plates or the popular and common paper toy soldiers.

These early figures are of great historic interest, representing as they do the first stage in the evolution of the commercial metal toy soldier. Their primitive design qualities create a strange dichotomy between cartoon and reality lending them the charm of the age which produced them (Figs 5 and 6).

The first manufacturer whose work can be positively identified and dated is Johann Gottfried Hilpert, a tinsmith who was born in Coburg. He set up his business mass producing a variety of metal toys in Nurnberg about 1770. Starting with civilian figures he eventually encompassed the theatre, farming, hunting, wild birds and animals, including a charming set of monkeys. There was none of the crudity about Hilpert's figures generally apparent in the pieces of earlier makers. They were beautifully conceived and characterised by expert engraving and casting. Hilpert and his family then turned to the contemporary military scene producing a series of 40 types of Frederick the Great's armies. These pieces are between two and three inches tall and were the beginning of a range which expanded rapidly to include the troops of many other nations.

Without question the most publicised and most sophisticated of Hilpert's productions is the beautiful mounted portrait figure of Frederick the Great, signed and dated 1777 on the base (Fig 7). There were others in the series, none quite so large or displaying the high

Figure 4
Flat metal soldier. German early 18th century. 160mm.

Figure 5
Flat metal colour bearer. Strasbourg mid 18th century.

Figure 6
Flat metal cavalryman. Strasbourg mid 18th century.

I Hand coloured paper
drummer, English, *c*. 1837.

II British line infantry,
German flats, *c*.1840.

III Flat Horse Guard by
J E DuBois of Hanover,
c. 1870.

Figure 7
Flat metal portrait figure
of Frederick the Great by
Hilpert. Signed and dated
J.H. 1777. 150mm.

Figure 8
Flat metal portrait figure
of Prince de Ligne by
Hilpert. 1780. 128mm.

artistry of the Frederick figure, but the Prince de Ligne (Fig 8) and Voltaire are both worthy of mention.

All of these figures, and their successors to the present day, were cast in moulds consisting of two flat pieces of slate with extremely smooth inner surfaces. The two sides of a figure were engraved one on each piece and precisely opposite each other. A conical entry hole at the top led into the engraving, and a multitude of tiny hairline channels emanated from it to allow air to escape as metal flowed through (Plate 1). In order to cast a figure the two pieces of the mould were clamped securely together and metal was poured in at the top. After the almost instantaneous solidification, the mould would be opened and the excess metal or 'flash' cleaned off the casting.

Early figures were cast from a high tin content alloy which was in later years further debased with lead. There was a sound technical reason for this: it created a metal which flowed into the mould more easily, and there was a sound business reason: it was less expensive.

The toy soldier was usually retailed either as a white metal casting, unpainted, or partly painted. Partly painted figures created a strange convention whereby the clothing and flesh of a figure were coloured, but not the horse or stand which both remained shining silver. There were of course exceptions to this rule, and ocassionally one sees a completely painted figure perhaps by Hilpert, coloured with extreme care and taste.

Generally speaking the painting of figures left much to be desired in terms of accuracy of colour and deftness of brushwork. Bulk painting was organised either by the maker or the retailer, and much of it was done by women working at home on a very low rate of pay.

Having been cast in their thousands, the figures were then wholesaled by weight in parts of a pound. Two and four ounce boxes would contain one type of troops, infantry, cavalry or artillery in various postures. Eight ounce and one pound boxes would have a mixture of these with probably some trees, bushes or bits of ruined building thrown in to add interest and make up weight. Or they might instead be made up of guns, limbers, waggons and caissons. The numbers per box for 25mm figures was something in the region of: two ounces, 36 foot or 16 mounted; four ounces, 72 foot or 32 mounted; eight ounces, 144 foot or 64 mounted; one pound, 288 foot or 128 mounted.

They were initially retailed in little oval boxes made from thin split pinewood. On the top surface they bore a printed paper label giving the maker's name, the contents (often handwritten), and showing medals won at various toy fairs.

Eventually the Hilpert's range of figures became so extensive, and collecting these little toy soldiers had become such a popular pastime, they were able to put together a lengthy catalogue of their products. The firm in due course was taken over by Johann Ludwig Stahl who issued his first catalogue in 1805. Under his ownership the quality of the figures began to deteriorate seriously.

Inevitably there was competition to fill the needs of this rapidly expanding market. Many other German towns such as Berlin, Luneberg, Wurtemberg and Leipzig developed their own thriving toy soldier industries and the city of Furth overtook Nurnberg as the main centre of production.

From about 1760 other European countries besides Germany and Italy began to foster their own toy soldier manufacturers. Amongst them Sweden, Switzerland, Denmark and Portugal were in the forefront. Production in these countries was not large; it appears that

3 Flat bandsmen by Bünau & Schundler of Leipzig c.1850. 30mm.

none were able to satisfy home demand. The Germans led the field, and between the last quarter of the eighteenth century and the first quarter of the nineteenth there was a continuing and rapid growth in the number of manufacturers contemporary with and immediately following the Hilperts.

Some because of the size of their business or the quality of their figures stand out from the rest. Antoine Joseph Bergmann who set up business in 1800 in Strasbourg, better known for its paper soldiers, had amongst his several hundred moulds the armies of Louis XV and Frederick the Great. Johannes Gottleb Lorenz started in Furth in 1800, as also did Johann Christian Allgeyer. Allgeyer's son Johann Friedrich became in later years the best known of the family. A fully fledged engraver, he was the first to put the family name on their figures. Using his expertise and training he personally contributed to the finish and quality of the firm's moulds. The Allgeyers made

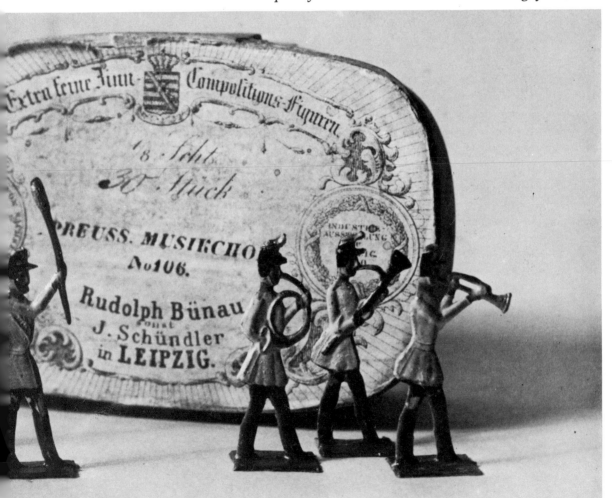

soldiers from many of the great periods of world history and included pieces of transport, guns, limbers and caissons in their repertoire.

Rudolf Wehrli in Aarau about 1830 produced a variety of military and non-military pieces including a circus, wild animals and representatives of the Swiss Army. Also in the early years of the century were Carl Weygang in Gottingen whose military pieces were good but rather scarce, and the Denecke family in Brunswick well known for their Napoleonic troops. The moulds belonging to one branch of the Denecke business were bought by Gebruder Reiche who started in Hanover about 1806. Reiche made the usual wide range of figures from medieval to modern, and the firm continued in business until the Second World War. Another maker, G Sohlke in Berlin, spread his effort across the field of military figures to railway engines, hunting scenes and nursery-rhyme characters.

In Nurnberg the three main makers were Christian Schweigger who set up in business in 1763; Johann Wolfgang Ammon in 1794 producing a range of Napoleonics, post Napoleonics of all kinds and an attractive series of knights in a tournament and J Wilhelm Gottschalk who started in Furth but later moved to Nurnberg.

Many of the businesses which were started in the late eighteenth century onwards survived well into the nineteenth and twentieth centuries. This was generally managed by a mixture of family interests or amalgamation with more stable and like-minded competitors. One outstanding case is that of Adam Schweizer of Diessen-Ammersee who opened up in 1796 and by the involvement of a succession of relatives the business still operates today under the ownership of Babette Schweizer.

The battles of the French Revolutionary Wars, and their European, Russian and Spanish aftermath provided toy manufacturers with a further wealth of source material. There were numerous campaigns, battles, regiments and personalities worthy of reproduction in miniature. The manufacturers tackled these offerings enthusiastically and produced large quantities of soldiers with varying degrees of visual success. It is not surprising that the post Napoleonic period saw a surging growth in the number of these manufacturers.

The most outstanding of them were Bunau and Schundler about 1840 in Leipzig. They made a broad selection of Napoleonic French, Prussians, British and other soldiers, not only the fighting troops but also some very attractive bandsmen (Plates 3 and 4); Johann Haffner in Furth in 1838 with his rather rigid figures of the Napoleonic period and the Franco-Prussian War; J C Haselbach in Berlin about 1848 who produced very good figures of various European armies, including the Crusades from a reputed stock of 5 or 6000 moulds; the superb quality of engraving reached by J E DuBois who opened his business in Hanover in 1830. In the field of flats he was best known for his German troops and ranges of lively and exciting ancients.

The most prominent of all these companies making flat toy soldiers was started by Ernst Heinrichsen in Nurnberg in 1839. It was destined to raise the industry to a new peak of achievement. Heinrichsen started by making the stock lines of soldiers, knights, farm and wild animals, religious scenes and hunts. The first soldiers he tackled were types of the contemporary German army. From that point his company ranged back and forth in time making pieces from the Napoleonic Wars (Plates 5 and 6), the Thirty Years War, the Russian Wars against Japan and Turkey, the Crimean War, the Indian Mutiny, the Boer Wars and others. Figures representing the combatants in the First and Second World Wars were all made into this century, production eventually ceasing about 1945.

The firm used drawings and paintings by top flight artists and draughtsmen as reference for the design of their products. This resulted in consistent accuracy of uniform and anatomical detail. One of the notable features of the Heinrichsen range is the obvious effort to make the soldiers realistic and active, a great enticement for the intending purchaser. This was further helped by the creation of large camp scenes and groups made up from specially designed figures. These groups formed a growing part of the production pattern and went a long way to help Heinrichsen achieve the eminence he enjoyed in the toy soldier field.

Toy soldiers became such a popular plaything that Ernst Heinrichsen wrote a book for children on how to conduct their armies,

4 Flat bandsmen by Bünau & Schundler of Leipzig c.1850. 30mm.

entitled *Kriegspiel*. And it was he who, tiring of the disparity in the sizes of toy soldiers, brought into being about 1848 a constant scale size of 30mm. The height was measured from the base to the top of the head of a hatless man, on foot. Quite predictably this suggestion was not immediately followed by all his competitors. Each had his own traditions and a high financial investment in thousands of finely engraved moulds. It has now become the standard size for most modern pieces, with the obvious benefit to the collector that the products of different manufacturers can quite happily be mixed.

By the closing years of the nineteenth century the toy soldier business was at its height. The elaborate groups and scenes involving anything from half-a-dozen to thousands of figures, with all the added paraphernalia of buildings, transport, large weaponry and vegetation were becoming quite commonplace. They were sold in oblong wooden boxes with sliding lids, generally covered with printed paper depicting either a colourful scene to be built with the contents, or a more sombre black and gold decorative design. Like their smaller counterparts these boxes displayed the medals won at toy fairs.

The Germans were exporting very large quantities of figures to America, Britain, Belgium, France, Holland, Norway and Sweden. Some of these little pieces began to change quite perceptibly in appearance from the clumsily painted, stylised objects of earlier days, to accurately uniformed gems of craftsmanship with perfect animation. The quality of painting and the ranges of figures increased as a result of business competition.

5 Gun team and Caisson by Heinrichsen of Nurnberg *c*.1840. Mounted figures 38mm. The base of the trumpeter is signed E.H.

In Britain, Grey's Cigarettes about 1932 produced two series of figures depicting the Battle of Waterloo and the Crimean War. They are of good quality and well detailed (Plate 10). There is a British Light Dragoon of 1800 almost certainly cast at a later date. The maker of this charming little horseman is unknown (Plate 11). During the twentieth century the flat figure has been pushed into fresh military avenues in an increasingly sophisticated and well-developed form. This has been achieved in part by the collectors whose requirements sway the market away from popular lines and into minor campaigns and little-known wars or ancient peoples about whom there is scant knowledge.

The engravers and designers of these pieces are now given just as much prominence as the makers. Ludwig Frank (1890–1957) cut moulds for many manufacturers such as Heinrichsen, Beck, Neckel and Spenkuch, and the services of the Maiers, father and son, are universally sought. Two internationally famous military artists who contributed to the design of flats were Richard Knotel (1857–1914), a German painter who also illustrated regimental histories and books

6 Flat Prussian Infantry by Heinrichsen of Nurnberg c.1840. 34mm.

on uniform, and Lucien Rousselot (1900–) a contemporary artist and illustrator. Rousselot painted the series of cards 'Uniforms of the First Empire' published by Bucquoy, and has collaborated in the illustration of a string of military publications.

The bigger manufacturers and distributers like Aloys Ochel of Kiel, Neckel of Stuttgart and Beck of Cassel have catalogues listing many thousands of pieces representing almost every conceivable military event and many civilian ones. Individual figures are often available in a variety of postures allowing, for instance, an infantry-man to be running, attacking, firing in three or four positions, loading, marching, being wounded, lying dead or casually smoking a pipe. Some 'combination figures' have two or three extra limbs, their selective removal allowing the collector or diorama maker added variations.

One of the great names in flats in this century is that of the late Otto Gottstein, a native of Leipzig who eventually moved to London. Originally a collector, he was later involved in the making of flat and solid figures at every stage of the production process. Gottstein's impact on the design of flats was tremendous, and in collaboration with Carman and Barnes he produced a series named Carbago which were made in Britain. He is best known for his work on a series of dioramas 'The King's Armies Through the Ages'. They were princi-pally made up from flats, and housed until recently in the Royal United Services Institution Museum in London.

By no stretch of the imagination can the flat soldier now be called a toy. He has developed into an exquisite model, painted or unpainted. Suitable for display singly or in groups or diorama form.

7 Mounted flats made in Germany c.1850. Lancer 43mm.

8 Mounted flats made in Germany. 44mm.

9 Colour party made in Germany *c*.1860. 34mm.

Identification

The flat tin soldier is well described by its name, and has only minor heightening for details and accoutrements. It might be engraved on one or both sides but is rarely more than 1mm in total thickness.

Normally having acquired some, it is desirable both to identify the makers and if possible date them. In the case of early pieces identification all too often can only be very sketchy, perhaps with luck naming the country of origin.

There is a general lack of information either in the form of marks on the figures or contemporary documentary evidence. One of the other possible recognition factors, the design style, is not reliable as designers and engravers were often employed at the same time by different manufacturers. A chart has been compiled by one toy soldier authority, Paul Martin, which links the shape of bases to their makers. This method has only limited use ignoring as it does the large body of pieces which defy any efforts at simple classification. Base shapes were rarely similar even within a single group or scene.

Hilpert initialled and dated some of his pieces, for instance one of the portrait figures of Frederick the Great has J.H. 1777 on its base. The Allgeyers put their name on the base as did Ammon and Heinrichsen. Sometimes they were varied by the addition of initials, occasionally it consisted only of initials. Gottschalk used the initials or name of his engraver F.Eggiman, Carl Wollrath and the Deneckes both used W.D. Carl Weygang used a selection of initials and one

10 Figures from the Battle of Waterloo and the Crimean War issued in Britain with Gray's cigarettes *c*.1932. 40mm.

might find C.W.G. or C.W. or W. or F.W. Confusion is caused by these and other makers who would quite inexplicably omit to put anything at all.

Obviously the named or initialled figures are most helpful, making identification easier and more positive. Gradually as a collection builds up cross checking of paint colours, painting techniques, base shapes and engravers and designers styles becomes possible. By handling and looking at many pieces a body of knowledge and an instinct for relating bits of information is developed. Figures which were of dubious or unknown background often fall into place, and can be confidently labelled or at least given a healthy attribution.

The manifold problems of identification are further complicated by a recent practise of re-casting from old moulds. How pleasant it would be to have the replica of a figure to be seen only in a museum. But how confusing for the historian or a future buyer unable to assess the true age and value.

11 British Light Dragoon, probably British made from a mould of 1800. 43mm.

3 Semi-Solids

The Transitional Toy Soldier

The cast metal toy industry was engaged from time to time in efforts to discover an alloy, less expensive and more easily worked than those with a traditionally high tin content. As far as toy soldiers were concerned this kind of change would have two other major benefits. Firstly to reduce the unit cost per figure thereby allowing more to be made for the same financial outlay. Secondly to produce a more realistic three-dimensional figure, which in tin would be prohibitively expensive and difficult to cast to a constant high standard.

Many of the manufacturers' experiments were centred round the

12 Semi-solid trumpeter, lancer and officer of a British regiment made by Allgeyer of Fürth c.1890. 36mm.

two cheaper and more easily obtained metals, lead and antimony. This progressed in due course to a general introduction of alloys containing a much higher percentage of lead.

In order to allow this new alloy to flow easily and also to achieve greater realism, castings were made bulkier. This gave the figures a new, almost three-dimensional appearance. Unlike the alloys with greater tin content, a soft lead mixture does not permit high quality detail to be reproduced. So although semi-solids have more 'body' than flats, they possess a lot less of the intricate engraving and fine definition. As toys they have two distinct advantages. A tendency to bend rather than break and relative cheapness compared to flats. The main disadvantage was the increased risk of children contracting lead poisoning.

Many years before the semi-solid was produced, some solid three-dimensional figures were made in France. It is not known whether they were made on a commercial basis, or were just an isolated pocket of activity. However as we are attempting to follow the main production trends, it is true to say that semi-solid toy soldiers followed the flat and preceded the solid. It therefore may be considered as a transitional toy soldier, and as such plays a most important role in the overall development. Its heyday was short, covering a span of some 10 years, before it was pushed into the background by the true solid toy soldier.

As with its predecessor the flat, once the semi-solids made by reputable manufacturers had achieved some status on the commercial market, there was an unusually vigorous effort by imitators and pirates. The general quality of these pieces was bad. Many of them plunged to a new aesthetic low. Without the kind of surface craft possible in flats, a poor semi-solid has little or nothing to offer.

The inexorable trend towards solids had, and still has, a few notable exceptions. Some makers saw the semi-solid as the ultimate stage in toy soldier design. These people usually had a higher tin content in their metal, thereby achieving a quality of detail and movement more reminiscent of flats.

As the majority of manufacturers were situated in Germany so the bulk of semi-solids emanated from that country. The British and French, as in the production of flats, do not appear to have had any keen involvement in the new figures. Sweden was more enthusiastic, and the United States may have dabbled tentatively but the evidence is not conclusive.

14 Gun team and spare wheel limber made by Allgeyer of Fürth c.1890. 34mm.

The Makers

15 Semi-solids perhaps of French manufacture c.1880. Foot figures 38mm.

To put a finger accurately on the name of the first maker of semi-solids, or on the date of production is impossible. It can be said that about 1850 Johann Haffner of Furth was making them, and he must have been closely followed or preceded by the other major manufacturers, Allgeyer (Plates 12, 13, 14), Ammon, Heinrichsen, Schweizer (Colour Plate VI) and Söhlke. Production revolved round the traditional themes, military scenes, bands, gun teams, ambulances, pontoons, railways and animals. Many of the wheeled vehicles were made of tin, some with extremely delicate cast-metal wheels. Soldiers of many nations were made in a variety of fighting and parade postures, complete with officers, colours, bandsmen and the other necessary arms of the service. At least one manufacturer, Allgeyer, duplicated many of their flat designs in semi-solid form.

Some of the strange conventions and mistakes from flats strayed into semi-solids. The most obvious ones were Scottish Highlanders with ridiculously short kilts; blobs of metal smoke appearing from the muzzles of firing guns; and much to the indignation of purists, Household Cavalrymen on brown horses. Georg Heyde, a maker who was eventually to become one of the biggest names in the toy soldier world, started producing semi-solids in Dresden about 1870. He created an extensive range displaying a high standard of quality and presentation.

A contemporary Austrian firm, Wollner, specialises in figures of the Franz Josef period (1848–1916). Including many large scenes of the Austrian Army on manoeuvres, cars and landaus with Austrian dignitaries, and bands of the infantry, cavalry (Plate 18) and artillery. Wollner together with Babette Schweizer, whose superb pieces of the Franco-Prussian War include many poignant little groups of two or three figures, form the backbone of current European semi-solid production.

In Sweden the foremost maker was Santessonska Tenngjuteriet of Stockholm whose business lasted from 1843 until 1930. In France the firm of Figur is well known. In the United States the St Louis Lead Soldier Company and Comet Metal Products have both produced semi-solids, while Swedish African Engineers (SAE) in South Africa currently have an extensive catalogue covering many periods and including three-dimensional guns and equipment.

The home casting of semi-solids was a popular hobby between the two world wars and many boy's papers carried advertisements for moulds. A new range of do-it-yourself moulds has recently come on to the market from Sweden, and the results are quite pleasing.

Identification

As a transitional piece the semi-solid contains elements of both flat and solid soldiers. A simple set of rules for the classification of true semi-solids would be:

Semi-solid horse and rider, single casting
Semi-solid horse, separate rider sometimes bent to animate, two castings
Semi-solid foot, sometimes bent to animate, single casting

16 Semi-solid band of a British Guards regiment made in Germany *c*.1900. 34mm.

17 Semi-solid band made by Gebruder Schneider of Leipzig, *c.*1910. 65mm.

The simplest test to ascertain whether a piece is a semi-solid or not is to view it from the front or rear, when the legs of a horse or man will be seen to be on a single plane. It therefore follows that semi-solids will always have a base to achieve the necessary stability. Flats reach a thickness of approximately 1mm, semi-solids take over at that point and vary between 1 and 10mm. This of course is a general guide and there are always exceptions.

One of the most curious steps in the transition from semi-solid to solid is the maker's habit of putting solid riders on semi-solid horses. Strangely enough this odd combination works very well and neither horse nor rider look out of place.

If the identification of flats might be considered difficult, the semi-solid is even more so. There are a few by known makers, and an absolute minority which bear any mark of identification. There is a multitude of pieces by unknown makers many of which were pirated. Unprotected by any form of copyright laws there was nothing which could be done to prevent it. It has left a chaotic and virtually uncataloguable situation.

18 Semi-solid Austrian cavalry band made by Wollner of Vienna, *c.*1970. 38mm.

Figures bought in their original boxes may with luck have a manufacturers name on the label. But a cautionary note here because it is common to find figures in the wrong box. Otherwise reliance on the advice of a reputable dealer is the only recourse, until years of experience and comparisons and cross checking allow a stab at classification to be made.

4 Solid Toy Soldiers

French Solids

To the Germans went the credit for giving us the flat and the semi-solid, two forms of toy soldier which found little or no favour outside the country of their innovation. To the French must go the credit for producing the solid.

It did not, as far as is known, evolve in France from the other less round forms of soldier but appears to have begun as a solid in its own right. It is not hard to imagine how rapidly these remarkably lifelike toys were accepted by children, making the flat and the tentatively accepted semi-solid redundant very quickly. Solids were of course considerably more expensive and for some years would only be bought by families of some financial substance.

19 Solid gun team of French Napoleonic Artillery by Lucotte of Paris, c.1870. From the collection of the Duke of Marlborough and on show in Blenheim Palace.

In the Musée de Cluny, Paris, there are a number of completely three-dimensional toy soldiers which were dredged up from the River Seine. They have been dated by the museum as belonging to the seventeenth and eighteenth centuries. From these rather corroded specimens to the point of naming makers there is no trace of a thread of continuous development. In common with the Germans the beginnings of commercial production in France are decidedly woolly. Once again the lack of any records or catalogues poses problems of identification and continuity.

It would be surprising however if after the French military exploits of preceding years, there had not been a crop of successful toy-soldier makers recording the deeds, the men and the glory. One or two people did work in Paris making the usual small metal charms and other trinkets, but there is no surviving evidence that they also made soldiers.

The first name of which we can be certain, is that of Lucotte who started making soldiers in Paris about 1790. There is a very large body of work bearing Lucotte's mark of the Napoleonic Imperial Bee flanked by the letters L and C still in existence, both in private hands and in museums. They are almost without exception the later Lucottes cast long after the firms incorporation by Cuperly, Blondel and Gerbeau (CBG) which in turn was absorbed by Mignot about 1875. Most of the figures bearing the Lucotte mark date from the period of the Mignot takeover. It is therefore fairly obvious that CBG Mignot continued to produce a range of Lucotte figures at the same time as their own.

The most prolific castings from Lucotte moulds are the French Army of the Revolution and the Grande Armée of the First Empire (Plates 19, 20, 21), (Colour Plates VII–IX). But they continue to cover the uniforms of French troops until the turn of the nineteenth century.

Every arm of the service is there, lancers, hussars, carabiniers, dragoons, guard and line infantry, the various regiments of artillery and transport. There are also foreign regiments in French service and regiments of the British army (Colour Plate X). They all have their officers, trumpeters, drummers and colour bearers. The bandsmen both foot and mounted readily catch the eye, prominent amongst them are the trumpeter of the Empress Dragoons and the Kettle-drummer of Carabiniers. Lucotte also produced a range of pieces depicting Napoleon and his staff.

There is a most attractive set of French Engineers illustrated in *Model Soldiers, a Collector's Guide* by Garratt. The caption informs us that they are dressed in white coats with scarlet trousers and kepis. It is interesting to note that this set is currently available from CBG

Mignot (without the Lucotte mark), wearing a more up to date First World War uniform of khaki and flat cap.

Lucotte managed to give his pieces a degree of anatomical refinement lacking in so many other solids. They exude a feeling of their period which is fostered not only by the excellent painting but also by the stylised poses of both men and horses. The most active of them retain a somewhat formal look.

The Parisian firm of CBG Mignot, now the oldest toy soldier firm still in production, has a vast range of some 20,000 moulds at its disposal. Having been in business continuously since before 1800 it is inevitable that their pieces form the backbone of many European collections. They are brightly painted and visually compelling seen either in small groups or *en masse*. Being solid and slightly heavier than most they are consequently very pleasant to handle (Plates 22, 23, 24, 25).

There are six distinct ranges of figures which can be bought. These come in a variety of packs containing different quantities. The most elaborate of Mignot's boxes is a three-tiered construction which allows three rows of soldiers or civilians to be positioned, together with relevant items of equipment. The inside ends and back of each tier are covered with a printed scene creating an attractive and sometimes appropriate setting. Other similar boxes are reductions from three to two or even a single tier. Mignot also sell small groups of their pieces in a simple rectangular bent card pack of bottom, sides and back held together and protected by a celluloid sleeve. Larger single soldiers are sold in differently shaped versions of this simple but

20 French and British infantry figures of the Napoleonic period by Lucotte of Paris, *c*.1870. From the collection of the Duke of Marlborough and on show in Blenheim Palace.

46

effective pack. All the pieces are either sewn or very solidly glued to the bases of their packs.

The most basic and inexpensive range of figures are made of an almost unbreakable aluminium alloy. They do not cover a very wide range of nationalities or military types, perhaps reflecting most accurately the interests of a young child in France. There are the old favourites, cowboys and Indians, available in all the usual firing positions; Ethiopians with spears; the Papal Swiss Guard; and a selection of figures from the modern French army including the Presidential Escort, St Cyr Cadets, Matelots and others all with various officers and buglers.

A range of 30mm concentrates mainly on the French army from Joan of Arc to modern times with the expected dominance of Revolutionary and First Empire troops, and a series of ancients which includes some excellent Romans. There are also hollow-casts of poor quality and a small series of 45mm solids depicting medieval and ancient times.

21 French Napoleonic Horse Grenadier by Lucotte, c.1870. From the collection of the Duke of Marlborough and on show in Blenheim Palace.

47

Mignot however are best known for their extensive range of 54mm solid figures. They lack the character and individuality of Lucotte's work, showing less flair in posture and design, but because of this and their shiny finish they evoke even more the image of the toy soldier.

The ancient world ranges cover all the more prominent peoples. Assyrians; Egyptians armed with shields, axes, clubs or spears; Franks; Greeks wearing the traditional Corinthian helmet and carrying large round shields, armed with spear or sword; Gauls covered in bearskin cloaks, armed to the teeth with double-headed axes, swords and spears; Romans, with officers of high rank, centurians, legionaries, signifers, cornicers and even lictors with fasces.

Pieces from the Middle Ages are mainly to be found in the slightly smaller scale of 45mm, but some knights on horse and on foot are made in the larger size together with relevant Saracen adversaries. There are some very colourful figures from the Field of the Cloth of Gold when King Francis I of France met King Henry VIII of England. From slightly later times there is the army of Henry IV and some well known Musketeers with their standard bearer.

The French infantry regiments from the period of the early and middle eighteenth century are well represented. Famous names from battles in America and Europe, de la Reine, de la Sarre, de Champagne, Royal Roussilon, march proudly in their white uniforms with distinctive coloured facings, boxed usually in fives. These troops are provided with officers, drummers, colours etc and are amongst the most attractive produced by Mignot. There are also cavalry regiments

22 A group of solid French infantry figures by CBG Mignot of Paris, c.1940. 54mm. Left to right, Revolutionary Infantry, Napoleonic Marines and 18th century Infantry.

4 Flat camp scene,
probably by Heinrichsen
of Nurnberg, *c.* 1880.

V Flat cavalry trumpeter,
German, *c.* 1870.

23 A solid WWI machine gunner by CBG Mignot, *c*.1920. 38mm.

with their mounted officers and standard bearers, and an extension to this range is provided by some American regiments of the period. Moving on in time to the Revolution, an extremely attractive set of infantry marching behind their drummer, in red white and blue striped trousers, has great character.

As usual there is a preponderence of pieces from the First Empire. They must rank as the most popular of all Mignot's lines, gay and colourful, representative of the sartorial height of French military fashion. Napoleon is available both mounted and on foot, with his staff which includes all the prominent Marshals of the Empire and their aides. The foot regiments of the Imperial Guard, soldiers, officers, drummers or buglers, sappers and colours. Of particular merit is the Third Regiment (Dutch) Grenadiers in their white uniforms faced with red. There are grenadiers à cheval and chasseurs à cheval with their exotically dressed trumpeters. Mamelukes and the famous First (Polish) and Second (Dutch) Lancers of the Guard. All the troops of the line are there too, officers on foot or horseback, private soldiers and bandsmen. The regiments of cuirassiers, carabiniers, dragoons à cheval and dragoons à pied, chasseurs à cheval, chevau-légers lancers and all the very colourful hussars are made. There are also ancillary arms like the marines, engineers and medical services.

Pieces of horse drawn equipment are most imposing and there is a good selection of guns, caissons and waggons drawn by different sized teams of horses. All the regiments of artillery are made for both the guard and line.

Nations allied to the French and those opposing them during the Napoleonic Wars are also in the catalogue. Dutch, Austrians, Russians, Prussians and British infantry and cavalry all receive a light coverage.

Moving on from the First Empire the next notable events in French military history were the Crimean War and the wars against Austria and Germany. French troops from these conflicts, infantry and cavalry, are produced, as are the best known of others, for instance the Russian Cossacks.

The First World War has been greatly elaborated on and the French infantry are cast in all the expected poses of the toy fighting man, aided and abetted by innumerable types of support facilities.

24 Solid Napoleonic lancer by CBG Mignot c.1970. 78mm.

There are soldiers marching with slung rifles; marching at the slope; charging with fixed bayonets; standing, kneeling and lying firing; operating automatic weapons; together with their officers, buglers and colours. Mignot's motor-cycle and pedal-cycle dispatch riders from this war give the feeling of being very precariously balanced on their machines, as do the chasseurs alpins on their skis. The band of line infantry in light blue coats, scarlet trousers and kepis is very gay and contains a bass drummer, cymbals, tubas, tenor horns, bell horns, side drums and saxaphones. It is headed by an officer carrying his sword at the salute.

Medical services are represented in a set which includes tables, couches, doctors and various recumbent figures well and truly bandaged. There are also sets of cavalry, general officers and sailors. The troops of other nations engaged in the conflict are made and one finds Russians, Germans, British, Greeks, Turks, Americans and others. As with the Napoleonics there is not quite the same breadth of personnel in sets of the opposing or allied armies. More of an outline representation of the basic infantry and cavalry units.

French, allied and opposing forces of the Second World War are extremely well catered for. Mignot in addition make an extensive

25 Solid Napoleonic
trumpeter by CBG Mignot
c.1970. 73mm.

range of personality figures from world history, soldiers, statesmen, kings and queens. These are produced on foot, mounted, or in pairs as most befits the subject; sometimes there is a choice. Civilian figures and public services are unfortunately few.

CBG Mignot have monopolised the French toy soldier market to the point where the names and products of other makers of similar metal solids have become submerged. Cherband, Berne and Figur are almost totally unknown in Britain, and the relatively small ranges of their pieces rarely find their way across the English Channel.

26 A selection of cavalry pieces by Heyde of Dresden, showing different sizes, qualities and categories of toy soldiers. Left to right; Life Guard, semi-solid man and horse, 50mm; officer 16th Lancers, semi-solid horse solid man, 62mm; Light Dragoon, solid man and horse, 50mm; King Edward VII, solid man on hollow-cast horse, 110mm.

German Solids

Unlike the French whose toy soldiers began life in a completely solid state, the early German manufacturers evolved the solid from a gradually thickening semi-solid. It is of course almost certain that they came into contact with, and were influenced by, French solids at the big European toy fairs held in Nurnberg, Leipzig and Paris.

The first of the major manufacturers who moved from semi-solids to the full round solid was Haffner of Furth, 1838–98 (Colour Plate XI). Quite unpredictably, what are believed to be amongst the first solid figures he produced about 1865 are of an exceptionally high standard – a quality which might have been expected only after numerous efforts and lesser productions. By the 1880s the firm's pieces were so outstanding in every quality that they had outstripped all rivals of any nationality. In a very short space of time they had reached the point where they were 'models of soldiers' rather than toy soldiers.

Haffner made figures representing most arms of the French and German Napoleonic armies, and continued to add a selection of pieces from contemporary conflicts mostly in 49mm. One of the best sets is that of the Emperor Franz Josef and his staff on horseback. His finest figures are not at all common either in auctions or from dealers and consequently command a high price when they can be found.

Germany did not take kindly to this three-dimensional revolution, preferring the more established home-produced flat. Not only was the flat cheaper and therefore could be amassed in thousands, but by the late 1800s they were attaining an extraordinary degree of anatomical and animational competence. Solids on the other hand were expensive, generally not so refined and compared badly on an aesthetic level. It is therefore all the more surprising that about 1870 one of the worlds most prolific producers and exporters of toy soldiers opened his business and flourished. Georg Heyde of Dresden made solids and semi-solids (Plates 26, 27, 28, 29, 30, 31). His pieces became famous the world over, and were exported from Germany in their millions. They were the most popular and common make of toy soldiers available both in Britain (Colour Plate XII) and America until the advent of the hollow-cast. Because they were so common they are often found to form, along with hollow-casts, the main body of pieces for collections of purely toy soldiers.

It was quite usual for boxed sets of toy soldiers to be made up from figures of a similar posture. These sets tended to be dull and uninteresting. Heyde with sharp business acumen exploited this situation, animating his figures into many postures he thereby created much more attractive boxes of soldiers. The boxed sets would be made up from different combinations and varying quantities of troops, and often included trees, shrubs and walls. One of the most exciting aspects of Heyde's productions is the number of scenic groupings he created; encampments, bivouacs, bands, hunts, gun teams, and numerous others. Pieces were made in an incredible array of qualities and sizes. The worst were mediocre, the best excellent and they could be in any of the five common sizes, 85mm, 75mm, 65mm, 54mm or 45mm. Heyde also made a variety of smaller pieces of irregular sizes, but for the majority of his output a 45mm standard was kept.

The list of different figures and sets is enormous and undiscovered in its totality. A selection of them will suffice to indicate the scope and variety once available from this manufacturer.

Working in a sporadic fashion but in chronological order of time the catalogue contains: Phrygians; Persians; Greeks; Germans dressed in cowhides or wolfskins, with a combined head-dress cum cloak topped by a set of horns; Romans, both legionaries and auxiliaries. They are all available in the wide range of postures which helped Heyde gain his reputation, marching, charging, standing, kneeling, slinging and holding shields, bows and spears. Each nation complemented by a related range of cavalry walking or galloping. A group from the Punic Wars comprises an elephant with houdah accompanied by warriors armed with bows, arrows, swords and spears.

The ancients are followed by Normans both foot and mounted and a remarkably broad range of medieval knights. They too are on foot

27 Solid cyclist by Heyde c.1910. 60mm.

or mounted, the horses caparisoned with head and neck armour and the men gaily decked with plumed or animal crested helmets. Many of Heyde's historical periods include pieces of differing sizes and qualities. The medieval period is no exception, and there are 85mm knights on foot protected by a shield and armed with spear or sword. Some have movable visors, and most unusually for Heyde, they also have movable arms.

Heyde's next most prominent period spans the middle and late eighteenth century. During this time the Seven Years War, the American War of Independence, and the French Revolution took

28 Wind-up musical band stand by Heyde c.1910. The mechanism causes the baton to move up and down. Figure 48mm.

29 Solid French
Cuirassier on semi-solid
horse by Heyde *c*.1900.

place. There are infantry and cavalry for the period, engaged in all
the variants of martial activity. Each unit with its officers on foot or
horseback, drummers, colour bearers and buglers. An artillery
battery has a mid-blue gun and limber, the gunners are dressed in
blue coats, white breeches, and black tricornes. A most attractive
and much illustrated bivouac scene from the American War of
Independence has soldiers sitting at table drinking from outsize
goblets; looking after a fire with suspended cooking pots; a line of
washing hung out to dry between two poles; men lying sleeping on
straw mattresses; a stand of flags and drums; and farmers with
bullocks.

The Napoleonic Wars are dealt with, not quite in the highly
individual regimental fashion of Mignot, but more simply with basic
uniforms. There is a great reliance on the variety of postures and
associated scenes to make the products commercially acceptable.
Some British Light Dragoons on splay-legged horses, their bellies
almost touching the ground must individually be amongst the most
charming pieces Heyde produced.

Both the Union and the Confederacy are well represented in the

56

30 Solid rider on semi-solid camel, British Camel Corps by Heyde c.1910. 74mm.

American Civil War series with cavalry, infantry and artillery. So is the Franco-Prussian War which might well have been going on at the same time as the founding of Heyde's business. It is not therefore surprising that the firm produced a good selection of pieces from this conflict. The expedition to the Sudan in a vain attempt to relieve Khartoum was a subject thought worthy of modelling. From the British Army in India came such exotic offerings as an elephant-drawn gun with seated gunners and camel mounted outriders.

There is a most fascinating series of scenes from the Boer War, apart from all the normal cavalry and infantry pieces. The Royal Army Medical Corps Group wearing khaki uniforms and tropical helmets includes a mounted officer, stretcher party and ambulance with seated driver, drawn by four semi-solid mules. An excellent pontoon section with a four-horse waggon, pontoon, planks, stanchions, oars and a mounted officer.

Gun teams were made mounted and limbered up, with gunners on foot serving the gun, as were more of the very precarious military cyclists. In the larger sizes Heyde made a 110mm mounted figure of Lord Kitchener in the uniform of a Field Marshal; Lord Roberts;

57

Edward VII; and a fine 70mm Prince of Wales in the uniform of a Royal Naval Captain.

The First World War has been extensively worked on, and a particularly interesting band of British Infantry wearing active service order and steel helmets contains officer, colour bearer, side drummers, cornets, tubas, tenor horns, cymbals, trombones and the bass drum. There are of course all the other combatants involved and one will find Germans, Americans, Turks, Russians, Indian Army and Spaniards. The full-dress uniforms of the British Army of the time were well produced. These included the Life Guards with their mounted band, the Royal Horse Guards (both occasionally on brown horses), lancers, hussars, dragoons, dragoon guards and the Royal Horse Artillery. The infantry was represented by the guards in varied postures with officers, colour bearers and their band. Infantry of the line in scarlet jackets and blue spiked helmets, the Rifle Brigade and Highland regiments also with their band.

Mention should also be made of the non-military aspects of Heyde's output, their South and North American Indians, African Warriors, Arab encampments and caravans, and civilians. Like Mignot in France, Heyde dominated the market in Germany until the early 1940s, when during the Second World War the factory was bombed and production ceased.

British and American Solids

Britain and America relied on the import of solids from Heyde and Mignot for their home toy markets. In Britain the solid toy soldier was not produced until a series of 20mm British and German Army and Air Force personnel were made about 1938 under the name of Skybird. At about the same time Richard Courtenay and W Y Carman both produced solids, but the intent, quality and cost of their pieces lifted them out of the toy category. Their efforts had foreshadowed the rise of highly detailed and perfectly animated model soldiers.

In the United States of America the pedigree of the solid toy soldier is a mystery. After the War of Independence with its consequent surge of loyalty to the new nation, children were able to obtain many more toys of American manufacture. Previously they had been imported from France and Germany. Toymakers were listed in the trade directories of most towns, and tin toys were popular during the second half of the nineteenth century. Many newspapers and journals carried advertisements for toy soldiers. It can only be presumed that all that was made has been lost, or that the pieces offered for sale were still foreign imports. The manufacturers names to appear with identifiable products were J L Wright of Chicago about 1910 and the St Louis Lead Soldier Company about 1920. Both of these manufacturers turned out products which compared badly with Mignot or Heyde.

Comet Metal Products of New York, a business started about 1938, made some semi-solids and solids. Although to begin with their figures were not of great merit this changed when the Swede Holger Eriksson was employed to design them. The name changed to Authenticast, the range expanded and the first large-scale commercial toy soldier venture was in successful operation.

Collectors in the United States however rapidly moved to a much more sophisticated product, and within a very short space of time a model soldier industry had blossomed. Spearheaded by Walter Imrie, Jack Scruby and Dr Bussler, their superb creations stand comparison with any models in the world.

Identification

A solid toy soldier is quite simply a casting filled all through with metal, and in order to differntiate it from a semi-solid it is fully three dimensional from any angle of observation.

Most solid toy soldiers have been designed and cast so that the basic body shape can be used for a number of different military units. This change from one unit to another, often of a different nationality, is facilitated by having plug-in heads and soldered-on equipment. Frequently a very soft metal is used, and a casting can be bent quite easily into a number of different postures. Bandsmen which would normally require a lot of expensive moulds become a viable proposition when it is only a matter of soldering on a number of

31 Solid Grenadiers by Heyde *c*.1925. Foot figure 53mm.

32 Typical lid from a box
of imported German
solids *c.* 1920.

different instruments. This crude method of animation usually explains why many figures have an odd anatomical structure and look incredibly stiff and inactive.

Horses for solid riders come in a variety of thicknesses from the true semi-solid through three dimensional solid to the hollow-casts which appeared in later years. These were imitative of the British hollow-casts, being cheaper to produce and lighter to export. The semi-solid horses always have bases, solid and hollow-cast horses may or may not. Riders of all these horses usually have a peg in the seat of their pants which corresponds to a hole in the horse's saddle, and prevents their falling off.

Precise identification of many early solid toy soldiers is difficult. All too frequently it is impossible to tell whether a figure is by Haffner, Heyde or one of the many pirate companies who copied their pieces and produced almost exact replicas. Or it might have been made by a small legitimate company whose name is lost to us and whose figures are consequently for ever unidentifiable.

Lucotte almost always stamped his products with an Imperial Bee flanked by the letters L and C. The bases might be painted a buff colour, the horses are long tailed in comparison to Mignot's short tail, the rider saddle and saddle cloth are all removable and the reigns are a separate casting. Mignot has the same buff base, but only the riders themselves are removable from horses and the reigns are cast in place. The paintwork on all these pieces varies from a slight sheen to very glossy. From the mid-1940s Mignot has stamped its pieces CBG MADE IN FRANCE.

George Heyde's figures have rather a long-bodied short-legged look, and of the three main manufacturers mentioned are the ones most obviously bent to shape. Close examination will show the point where the heads plug into shoulders, and rifles are frequently cast pouring forth metal smoke and flame. The larger Heyde pieces are better in the quality of their anatomy and painting. Some have refinements such as removable helmets and swords which slip out of their tiny tinplate scabbards. The largest mounted figures are usually seated on hollow-cast horses. Paint was both matt and gloss.

5 Wooden and Composition Figures

The Wooden Toy Soldier

Wood must rank, along with clay, as the oldest most commonly used toy-making medium in the world. It was accessible to all regardless of their financial or social status. Its modelling limitations were bounded only by the skill of the individual craftsman. From earliest times it has been carved and shaped with little effort and the cheapest of implements into representations of humans, animals, furniture, transport, architecture and vegetation.

Wooden figures, both toys and votive offerings, have been recovered from graves and dwellings in countries as far apart as Egypt

33 Musical Cavalry toy in painted wood c.1880. 130mm.

and New Guinea. They are usually painted and often clothed in garments made from cloth or grass. The realistically painted groups of Egyptian soldiers from the tomb of Prince Emsah who died during the Twelfth Dynasty are a good example.

In the middle ages, sophisticated hand operated jousting knights were made using a basic jointed wooden figure which was then clothed in a suit of metal and leather armour simulating exactly the protective battle wear of adults. Even the children of peasants could have had wooden toys, not so magnificent, probably not mechanically operational but none the less loved and cared for.

The Germans have an especially strong tradition of wooden toy production. Common everyday life, warfare and their particularly rich folklore form the groundwork and influences. There are some delicately carved and carefully observed soldiers from the period of Frederick the Great still in existence (Colour Plate XIII). The tradition springs mainly from the regions of the Black Forest and Bavaria which are heavily wooded. The Americans too have this background where home-made wooden toys were commonplace. It flourished there in areas where there was only a small community of pioneers and farmers. They created no demand for quantities of commercially produced toys and so made their own. In both those countries the wooden toy tradition had a profound influence on the design of mass-produced toys of later years.

During the Victorian era in Britain toys of all kinds were made from wood. Toy forts and soldiers, building blocks (where the image was printed on paper and glued on) were common as were turned wooden guardsmen skittles many of which had additions such as arms and guns. Other popular forms of military plaything were the scissors or trellis toy, and the simple mechanical drill toy which performed basic parade manoeuvres. They were operated by pushing, pulling or sliding strips of wood connected to each other by pivots and upon which toy soldiers were positioned. Others in a similar vein utilised a clockwork motor as the power source and perhaps even played a suitable military tune whilst functioning (Plate 33).

Most early wooden toys were privately made and can not be considered as serious commercial ventures. In the main detail tends to be more simple than that found on cast-metal figures. For that reason, and the slowness of production, wooden toy soldiers never became more than a novelty.

More recently the Czechoslovakians have produced little turned wooden figures freely resembling British guardsmen. They come in a bag complete with sentry box and trees. Soldier figures within figures and egg-shaped containers filled with soldier skittles are also made.

Wood has been used as a basis for the production of extremely sophisticated model soldiers, precisely reproducing every detail of the original uniform. Some are clothed in natural materials, have helmets and equipment which are removable and carry weapons made with the utmost engineering skill. Three of the main exponents of these sculpted figures are Eugene Lelièpvre, the late C D O Pilkington-Jackson and Helmut Krauhs. The late René North, who was well known for his uniform illustrations, produced many painted silhouettes of British and foreign regiments. This silhouette form of wooden soldier is quite common and may be seen frequently in military museums.

Wooden soldiers are very individual items, and cover such a long time span that it is possible to pick up some strange and fascinating items in antique and toy shops. Their value is entirely dependent on age and the state of preservation.

Composition Figures

Numerous concoctions of plaster, clay, even gingerbread and confectionary have been used to make toy soldiers. They have resulted in the bizarre, the amusing and in some cases realistic and highly detailed figures. One of the more popular is papier-mâché which has had a long run. Toy soldiers were commercially made in this substance, as far as is known, from about the end of the eighteenth century. The French call figures made from it 'carton-comprimé'.

In Germany, the home of many innovations in toy soldier design and production, a new idea was made commercially viable. It was a mixture of natural and easily obtained substances, the main ones being wood and glue. This remarkable venture was started by O & K Hausser in Neustadt about 1904. Their pieces were moulded over a wire armature and then finished off with a mixed water and spirit based paint. The resulting figures look heavy, details having to be exaggerated to show up sufficiently. They almost give the impression of being hand carved, which of course would make them very acceptable in a country with the wooden toy traditions of Germany. They were exported to Britain and America before the Second World War but did not achieve very great popularity. Their various sizes and general bulk made it impossible to integrate them fully into the firing line with flats, solids and hollow-casts.

Unlike some other prolific German toy firms, Hausser's factory was not put out of action during the war and production never ceased. Figures were still available in the composition substance when in 1958 a start was made with toughened polystyrene. In 1960 the modern military ranges were discontinued and Hausser went over entirely to plastic soldiers, civilians and animals.

Hausser's trade name is Elastolin and its well-illustrated catalogues covered many periods and nationalities. The figures themselves in the early days came in scales ranging from 50 to 300mm. This settled to 40 and 70mm in the late 1930s. Among the pieces they offered for sale was a most attractive medieval range. Knights in full and half armour carrying shields and fighting with swords, halberds, axes and maces. These knights were supported in their combat activities by pieces of contemporary medieval artillery.

An obviously popular line for most manufacturers, Hausser being no exception, was the Wild West. It was represented in its catalogue by dozens of figures. There were Indians both on foot and horseback, foot figures fought, danced, relaxed, smoked pipes of peace, or in the case of squaws cooked and looked after children. Chiefs and medicine men were there in a variety of postures, to lead the braves and stand guard over cowboy prisoners tied to stakes. The mounted figures in action poses are seated on the most vigorously moving horses. Others trot or walk very elegantly in a most peaceful and calm manner. All the items necessary for the creation of an Indian encampment were made, tepees, totem poles, camp fires, cooking fires with hunks of meat hanging over them, trees, bushes and rocky outcrops.

The cowboys were similarly treated and included a choice of sheriffs and very obvious bad-men looking extremely sinister. Mounted pieces are shooting with pistols and rifles, or swinging limp string lariats in the air. There was a nice selection of town and ranch buildings, stockades, log cabins and even covered waggons and an overland coach for the cowboys. One series of western figures had a locomotive and waggons accompanying them.

There was a range of soldiers from the early 1900s which featured a squat German infantryman at the slope wearing a picklehaub. British troops of the period included some elegant mounted lancers in full dress uniform whose horses are particularly well modelled (Plate 34). These larger-sized horses are set into wooden bases to give them added stability.

Between the two world wars production was continually on the increase, and the quality of casting was maintained to a high standard. The pre-Second World War German forces were given coverage in depth (Plate 35), and there are many groups of figures for the creation of scenes. The British Army was very well represented. Soldiers were available in all the activities and action poses which might be required in a drawing room floor battle. Other ranks stood, knelt and lay firing rifles; advanced with fixed bayonets; swung rifles like clubs; threw hand grenades; operated height or range finders; marched at the slope; signalled with flags or radios;

34 Elastolin figures of a British lancer, Life Guard and Horse Guard c.1920. Lancer 185mm.

played in bands; carried little canvas stretchers; used field telephones; fired heavy and light machine guns or were simply well-bandaged casualties. Officers read maps; walked with swagger sticks or binoculars; and carried colours. They were also available in some cases as mounted figures. There was an attractive group of the medical service, doctors, nurses and orderlies to tend the wounded (Plate 36). The whole was complemented by gun teams, artillery pieces and ambulances.

Many famous British regiments were portrayed in full-dress uniform, for instance the Coldstream Guards and the Gordon High-landers. Its respective series encompassed mounted and foot officers; non-commissioned officers; soldiers at the slope; colour bearers and bandsmen. The Highland regiments of course had full pipe bands.

One of the most attractive figures that Elastolin made was that of a Swiss soldier releasing a carrier pigeon while his dog looks on (Plate 37).

Its efforts to produce troops of different nations led it for instance to paint German castings in khaki to represent British troops, only the head of the mould being changed. This creates some strange and often amusing anomalies in equipment and uniform detail.

Elastolin did not stop at fighting man and their paraphernalia. Farmyard animals, wild animals, circus and zoo pieces have always formed a large and important part of the firm's range.

Another manufacturer active at the same time, and making figures of incredibly similar design and material consistency was Lineol of Dresden. At best its figures are extremely good but the general level is not as consistently high as Elastolin. A glance at a Lineol catalogue shows a remarkable selection of pieces. Perhaps most impressive is its portrayal of the German Army before the start of the Second World War.

Personality figures of Hindenburg, Hitler and his principal adherents including Goebbels, Hess, Goering, Raeder and Ludendorf were made. Many of them in different uniforms and with jointed arms which could be elevated into the Nazi salute. Mounted officers included generals, adjutants and junior commissioned ranks on walking horses or attacking waving their swords. There were also mounted infantry with their complement of officers and trumpeters on walking or galloping horses. A mounted band was made to add a musical touch to parades and other formal occasions.

On foot the different branches of the arm were each well rep-

36 Elastolin Royal Army Medical Corps and Casualties. Left to right; British nurse and wounded soldier; British stretcher party; German soldier wounded; German soldier helping a wounded comrade. Stretcher bearer 65mm.

69

resented. Officers were cast standing; marching; attacking; holding field glasses, maps, telephones, swords or colours. The other ranks, in the same basic postures as Elastolin, played every kind of musical instrument, fired all types of modern firearm, threw stick grenades, carried flame-throwers with solid jets of flame bursting from their nozzles, clanged gas alarm gongs, manned artillery pieces, climbed telegraph poles, drove trucks, carried wounded comrades or lay on the ground dead. Lineol devoted many of its pieces to special units such as the SA, SS, or Hitler Youth movement. These included bands, banners, officers, bearers of lighted torches and uniformed females.

One of the most unusual items in its catalogue deals with a trench system. It was built up from a selection of gun emplacements, some incorporating living quarters, and lengths of front line trench guarded by barbed wire entanglements. They were available in different lengths of straight and curved section allowing any shape to be put together, in the same fashion as the track on a model railway. This front line trench was reached by a series of sapping trenches constructed on the same principle, enabling a complete and realistic trench system to be easily constructed.

Wheeled transport was made from tinplate, and was a mixture of the earlier horse drawn vehicles and more up-to-date motorised versions. Different sized teams of wheeled horses pulled heavy and light artillery pieces capable of firing small missiles and amorce caps. There were also pontoon waggons, ambulances, field kitchens and general waggons. Motorised vehicles pulled guns or searchlights, mounted behind the drivers cab. Armoured cars, ambulances, troop carriers, *kübelwagens* and staff cars were made, each with its complement of drivers and ancillary personnel.

The pre-selected groups were extremely attractive and undoubtedly very commercial. Troops on the march, 10 pieces; troops on the march with a band, 18 or 20 or 29 pieces. These groups and others were sold with variations of standards and mounted officers. One particularly attractive selection of 20 pieces comprises 12 soldiers at attention, six soldiers at attention with standards, and a marching officer accompanying General Goering on an inspection. Artillery groups had a gun and varying numbers of officers, gunners, height finders etc. There was a general staff group; signals and telephone engineers groups; and a very un-Germanic bivouac set with the soldiers in most relaxed poses.

Lineol also made British troops in battle dress and full dress. As with Elastolin the kilted Highland regiments were well represented. Soldiers marching at the slope, officers saluting and marching with drawn swords, on foot or mounted, together with the inevitable pipe

37 Elastolin's Swiss Army
messenger pigeon being
sent off. 70mm.

bands. They made representatives of British Guards regiments and
other famous military bodies from other nations like the American
West Point Cadets.

The Elastolin and Lineol factories between them made the bulk of
composition figures. It was not an internationally popular business,
and although some were produced in France the largest quantity
manufactured outside Germany was in Italy. The Italian firm of
Xiloplasto, using a similar composition to Elastolin, made Wild West
figures, Union and Confederate forces and Canadian Mounted Police.
They later changed to a rubber material and produced more modern
soldiers and a series of ancients.

Identification

Composition figures are a particularly easy classification of toy
soldiers to recognise. They are chunky and look as if they have been
carved from wood, except that they are lighter. Very fine casting is

71

not possible with the manufacturing materials at that scale, so their bases are particularly thick and invariably have the maker's name cast in relief on the underside. The wire armature on which each figure is cast helps to give it strength. However the composition has a habit of splitting at the narrowest parts i.e. gun barrels, ankles, wrists and necks. This is an added, if undesirable and unfortunate, aid to identification.

38 A Britains' mould for the production of hollow-cast toys. The photograph shows one half of the mould with the entry spout for metal, rotated back, at the top.

VI Franco-Prussian War
group of semi-solids by
Babette Schwiezer of
Diessen-Ammersee, c. 1870.
cast from an old mould.

6 Hollow-Cast
Toy Soldiers

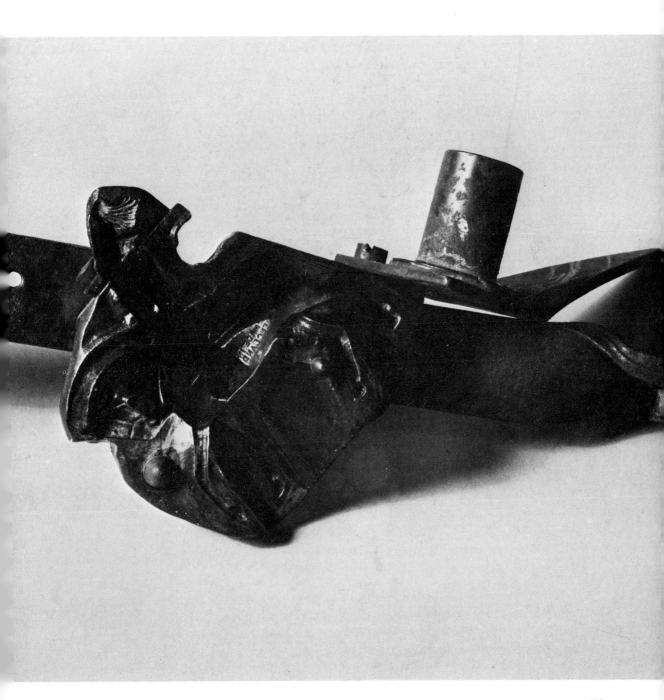

William Britain

During the last quarter of the nineteenth century, the British toy soldier market was presented with a selection of German and French products. These came mainly from the factories of Heyde, Heinrichsen and to a lesser extent Allgeyer, Mignot and Lucotte. The representation of British regiments from these people was not extensive, uniform detail was often wrong, but with that the purchasers had to be satisfied. Imported figures gained their popularity mainly because there was nothing else to choose from. The quantity of metal used in their manufacture and the high cost of import made them fairly expensive.

It was in this climate of European domination and exclusivity that the next, and most important, step in toy soldier development and manufacture took place. An Englishman bearing the memorable and apt name of William Britain adapted a process whereby he could produce hollow-cast toy soldiers. That is a casting which consists only of a metal skin, hollow in the centre.

William Britain had been involved in designing and making mechanical toys for some 50 years. Without doubt this ingenious and creative man had seen great commercial potential in the toy field, particularly in toy soldiers. His creations would be light in weight because of the sparing use of metal, making them much less costly on the home market and so available to a wider public. More important for his business aspirations, the inherent lightness of his figures would make them comparatively inexpensive to export.

His venture into toy soldier production was well timed in an historic sense as we shall see, this by a happy accident of fate rather than by design.

Military Influences

When William Britain first put his toy soldiers on to the market in 1893, the British Empire was at the height of its authority and prestige in the world. It encroached on every continent, extending territorially from Canada in the North to the Falkland Islands in the South, from Jamaica in the West to New Guinea in the East. For a tiny nation of approximately 30 million people, the British were territorially acquisitive and politically influential: a trading concern on the grandest scale.

Queen Victoria occupied the throne for some 64 years, the period of greatest imperial expansion. She was a seemingly permanent royal figurehead and the epitome of monarchical conservatism. Victoria was queen and empress to millions of people in many nations, and a direct relative of all the ruling houses in Europe. During her rule the

British nation grew in confidence and stature, a spirit of missionary idealism ran high. Her subjects had a strong sense of pride in national achievements and dutiful loyalty to the crown.

In 1837 the year of the young queen's ascent to the throne, British troops were in action in the field. From that year onwards a series of conflicts broke out which were to continue unceasingly for the rest of her reign. The British army were to be engaged in some 50 different wars, one or two of major importance, others no more than punitive expeditions. Balances of power were juggled with, insurrections were quelled and trade was protected. British foreign policy towards Europe during much of the nineteenth century was one of isolationism. This resulted in the army fighting all over the world, Afghanistan, Africa, Canada, China, Russia, India, everywhere except Europe. A very brief summary of some of these actions and the participants will help to illustrate the type of information which, appearing in the press, helped to direct public interest towards military toys.

After the successes of the Peninsular War and Waterloo, confidence in the capability of the army ran high. So when during the First Afghan War of 1839 it suffered one of its most disasterous reverses in the destruction of the Kabul garrison, the news media gave it headline treatment. This war trickled on until as late as 1880 when Lord Roberts defeated the Afghans at the Battle of Kandahar.

India was the scene of the heaviest military committment. About half the British army, which was entirely composed of volunteers, being on permanent station there. That continent saw a great deal of fighting, the Scinde War of 1843, the Sikh Wars of 1845 and 1848 where Sir Hugh Gough and Sir Harry Smith achieved the victories of Aliwal, Sobraon, Chillianwallah and Gujerat. In 1857 the Indian Mutiny broke out at Meerut, and in June of that year the Cawnpore garrison was massacred. Lucknow and Delhi were both besieged and later relieved. Many famous soldiers held commands during the mutiny; among them Sir Henry Havelock, Sir James Outram and Sir Colin Campbell (Lord Clyde) who on 6 December 1857 finally defeated the rebels at Cawnpore.

The Crimean War of 1854 was made memorable by a constant series of indecisive and inept manoeuvres, Florence Nightingale's attitude to nursing and later Roger Fenton's war photographs. British newspapers applauded the bravery of the 'gallant six hundred' men of the Light Brigade, who rode up a shot torn valley and back again. Or the highlanders who formed the 'thin red line' to stop an advance by Russian cavalry. There are many names associated with this war, Raglan, Cardigan, Lucan, Nolan and Campbell, few of whom come out with any credit.

There were troops in Canada during the American Civil War and

General Charles 'Chinese' Gordon campaigned successfully in China against the Taeping rebels.

Africa like India saw its fair share of the British army. Garnet Wolseley led an expedition against the Ashantees in 1874. On the 22 January 1879 during the Zulu War a massacre of British Troops took place at the Battle of Isandhlwana. Immediately following this bloodbath one of the bravest feats of British arms took place, the defence of Rorke's Drift. Seven Victoria Crosses were won when 132 men held off many thousands of Zulus. In July of that year the Zulus were defeated at the Battle of Ulundi by a force under the command of Lord Chelmsford.

Between 1880–81 the First Boer War saw more reverses for the British. Fighting against the guerilla tactics of the Boers, they were beaten at Laings Nek, Ingogo River and Majuba Hill.

The Egyptian War which involved the Bombardment of Alexandria and the Battles of Kassassin and Tel-el-Kebir took place in 1882. The British forces were commanded by Sir Garnet Wolseley. In 1883 the Mahdist uprising led to General Gordon being sent to Khartoum, where he was beseiged and eventually killed. Wolseley led an expedition up the Nile in a vain effort to relieve him and on 17–18 January fought the actions of Abu-Klea and Abu-Kru. The Mahdists were beaten in skirmishes from time to time. It was not until Sir Herbert Kitchener defeated them at the Battle of Omdurman that they were finally put down.

There were other minor campaigns in Africa, but the next most important was the beginning of the Second Boer War in 1899. Not only British regular soldiers were involved, but volunteer battalions and troops from all parts of the empire also took part.

This constant state of warfare brought acclaim and glory to men and regiments. It made memorable the exploits and the battles in which they fought. Drawings by war artists actually at the scene of the action, and later photographs gave the news a dramatic and realistic quality at home.

Who could fail to be impressed by Lord Cardigan, 'the last of the Brudenells', as he led his brigade towards the Russian guns in the Crimea; by Lieutenants Chard and Bromhead and the men of the 24th South Wales Borderers at the defence of Rorke's Drift; by the charges of the 17th Lancers at Ulundi and General Drury Lowe's heavy cavalry at Kassassin. The public followed with prayer and fervent hope Wolseley's effort to save the beseiged Gordon, and were shattered at the news of his death. Their opinion then put Kitchener on a pedestal after Omdurman when they read of the charge of the 21st Lancers, the relatively unknown Lieutenant Winston Churchill in their ranks.

Full dress uniform was in its heyday both at home and abroad. The infantryman still wore a red coat, lancers carried lances, hussars had heavily braided tunics, horses had not yet been replaced by tanks or bicycles. The army had a dual public image. In print it was inefficiently administered and poorly led, but on parade where it was most often seen bands played stirring tunes, bayonets glinted and colours hung heavy with battle honours. It caught and held the public interest, with all its trappings of magnificence and grandeur.

Queen Victoria would soon celebrate her Diamond Jubilee, troops and dignitaries from every corner of her empire would congregate in London.

William Britain put an attractive and relatively inexpensive line of British made British uniformed toy soldiers into the shops. His success was almost a foregone conclusion.

Britains Ltd & Their Products

William Britain's mechanical and engineering experience must have made the practical problems of hollow-casting a lot easier to deal with. It is a process which requires a great deal of skill and careful timing. The hand-held mould is made in two main halves, with the possibility of removing and replacing the head which is also in two halves (Plate 38). This allows for the creation of different regiments without much extra expense.

The two halves of the mould are clamped together, an entry spout is rotated into place and it is ready to accept molten metal. Now comes a critical point in the casting process. With the mould at the right working temperature molten metal is poured in, and then out again. It is the period of seconds between the metal going in and coming out that allows a thin outer skin to form in the mould. The metal in the middle must not be allowed to solidify or the figure would become an expensive and weighty solid piece.

Every Britains' figure was cast by hand as an individual item. Arms and other movable parts were then fitted and the toys hand coloured in gloss paint to an extremely high standard by women working at home. Original master figures from which the moulds were made were sculpted in wax.

William Britain & Sons Ltd, as the firm was called originally, did not get immediate acclamation for their new products. It took a lot of persuasion before the suspicious British toy trade would accept this odd new type of hollow plaything. It was Messrs Gamages in London who eventually took the plunge and gave some space over to them. Once on display the figures sold well and very quickly became a popular line. It was not long before a whole department was exclusively filled by Britains' hollow-cast toy soldiers.

The figures were attractively packed in boxes covered by an orange/red paper, which together with the large printed label gave them an exciting appearance.

Figures, in the main, were a standard height and there was an initial concentration on making representatives of regiments of the British Army. This was a popular move especially as the company also resolved to achieve as accurately detailed a figure as possible. The uniforms and physical characteristics of the prototypes were carefully studied before a metal miniature was put before the public.

There was no effort to create a multitude of postures for these figures, in fact Britains only made their infantrymen in a dozen basic attitudes. This, added to their concentration on the British Army, went down well with the younger generation. Columns and squares of troops, on parade or in action, could be easily built up by buying similar or complementary boxes.

The first figure was on the market in 1893, by 1895 there were 20 varieties of pieces available in similar lots or assortments. By 1905 there were over 100 different pieces, and a turnover of approximately 5 million castings a year. In 1908 Britains published a 16 page booklet entitled *The Great War Game for Young and Old*. Primarily intended as an advertisement for their toys, it preceded and may have influenced the publication of *Little Wars* by H G Wells.

In 1905 a French branch was opened, issuing figures not all of which appeared in Britain. The Britains' factory turned to the production of munitions during the First World War. This phased out toys for some years. When they were able to return to them, a general antipathy to war caused the company to expand by introducing some non-military lines such as their Model Home Farm series.

Re-armament in the 1930s awakened military interest once again and the firm introduced topical models of anti-aircraft guns, barrage balloons, searchlights and khaki-clad figures of the regular army, territorial army and home guard. By 1940 the catalogue of different lines and models was at its height. It would not have been possible to name a regular regiment in the British army that Britains did not make, as well as selected pieces from all the foreign armies. They even produced many of the British volunteer and Yeomanry regiments, and military school cadets.

During the Second World War the company again had to stop the production of toys, and throw their resources into the war effort. After the war metal was too scarce and precious for distribution on the home market, all the figures that were made had to be exported. The number of different regiments that were made was drastically reduced. Britains put a greater concentration on peaceful civilian lines which included railway personnel, passengers, farm and zoo animals, hunting scenes, the circus and boy scouts. These, and the soldiers, were cast in ever increasing quantities. By the 1950s it could still be fairly claimed that Britains were the largest toy soldier producing company in the world.

In 1954 Britains took the momentous step in incorporating Herald Miniatures into their operation. Herald plastic toys were the leaders in their field, and were made to a very high standard. They were the forerunners of Britains' ranges of plastic soldiers which were introduced from 1954 and continue to appear from time to time. The mid-1960s saw the firm's production of metal figures cease altogether. Plastic being substituted for all but artillery pieces and parts of wheeled farm vehicles. Between 1968 and 1972 even the depleted ranges of these plastic figures were reduced to a point where toy soldiers all but disappeared from the Britains' catalogue.

They have slowly re-introduced metal into their figures. At first a series was produced with metal bases, then the 1973 catalogue went a step further and showed a metal guardsman with only a plastic rifle and bearskin. In 1974 they brought a further two figures into the series. Collectors will now have to hope that the world's once premier toy soldier manufacturers will continue to enlarge this range.

From well before the First World War Britains were exporting millions of boxes of their figures to countries all over the world. These included Germany who had previously been the main British supplier, the United States of America, New Zealand and Australia where interest in their figures is keener than ever. This tremendously large overseas market is reflected in the leading place Britains' toy soldiers hold in most collections.

During the 80 or so years of metal toy soldier production, Britains made their figures in many different combinations of scale, sculptural and painting qualities. The different standards to which these pieces were made were reflected in the retail prices and often in the types of establishment selling them. At the lower end of the scale the pieces lacked any sparkle and were somewhat featureless, often the products of old moulds. As a consequence of dipping the figure rather than brushing it, the paint quality left a lot to be desired. These would normally be sold in the less expensive chain stores. The top grade lines of the standard size maintained a very high quality throughout the years. Hand painting, helped laterally by spraying, imparted a finer finish with a greater degree of detail. These could be bought at all the better toy shops.

An attempt to break down the sizes and ranges of Britains' figures is made difficult by conflicting evidence or lack of evidence. Constant anomalies occur such as catalogues naming ranges of figures which do not appear within their pages; or frequent discoveries of soldiers made by Britains which do not appear in their catalogues. The problem of whether they were ommitted by oversight or made for a private collection if often difficult to answer. It is possible however to put the sizes and ranges into a sequence of appearance.

In 1893 when the first figures were introduced, an infantryman was cast to a height of 54mm or the 'standard' size as Britains called it. This popular size was used for most of their productions and continues to be the measure for their soldiers today. The company during this first year of operation also produced a figure 70mm in height, this was later to be known as the 'H' range. During these early years, in fact up until 1896, all Britains' figures were cast with immovable arms. Cavalrymen had a sliver of tin as a sword, lances were originally cast metal but this was changed to wire in all cases by 1903. Britains cavalry figures were never removable from their horses. Infantry figures holding rifles had them plugged into their cuffs by means of an extended wrist. Figures of bandsmen had a slot cut on each side of the body, up at the shoulder. Into this arms with attached instruments were soldered. This practice continued until 1911 when an improved movable arm working on a swivel basis was introduced. It had been in general use for infantry and cavalry since 1896.

Also in 1896 Britains had introduced a further range, later to become the 'B' series, in which an infantryman was 45mm in height. By 1904 these pieces had all the high painting and modelling qualities of the 'standard' size top-grade figures. Shortly after, this excellent range was merged with and superceded by another range termed 'W'. The 'W' series did not measure up to the quality of the earlier 'B' series. They were all fixed arm and obviously intended for a cheaper market.

By 1905 there were a further two ranges 'A' and 'X', both of standard size. They were in turn merged into a new 'A' series. These 'A' and 'X' series were cast from earlier fixed-arm moulds which had been improved and re-issued with movable arms and better modelling. They had mostly kept the fixed arms and were painted as second grade.

The 1920s and early 1930s saw a further expansion in both sizes and ranges. There was, apart from the best quality, in standard size 'A', 'B', 'C', 'P' and 'Crown' series. Smaller sizes were also there in greater numbers being represented by 'W' and 'D' both 45mm, and 'M' at 47mm. Larger figures were made in 70mm which was termed 'H' and 83mm was termed 'HH'.

To sum up all the ranges in the 1933 catalogue. There were 54mm best quality packed in sets in the famous red boxes. An 'A' series of inexpensive second-grade figures also packed in sets. A 'C' series of second-grade figures packed in bulk to be sold as single items, and a 'P' series of sparingly painted second-grade pieces also packed in bulk. The smaller sizes were the 'W' series of 45mm figures which were packed in sets, and the 'D' series packed in bulk. The only larger size mentioned in this particular year is the 'H' series at 70mm. Certain selected regiments were sold as 'Parade' series from both the best quality and 'A' series of 54mm pieces. These figures were slotted into specially made cardboard bases in a marching formation. Each base containing nine figures.

There were further alterations in the ranges and the 1940 catalogue lists the best quality series, 'A' and 'N' series of second grade, all these being 54mm. The 45mm range contained two series 'W' and 'D'. Other sizes were the 47mm 'M' series, and the smallest size ever produced by Britains, 20mm, which were termed 'OO' and 'T'. By the 1950s the range of different sizes was much reduced, and soldiers were only made in the 54mm scale. They were obtainable in best quality, 'S' or 'P'.

When the company introduced plastic soldiers in 1954, they were the Herald range made in Hong Kong. A minor deviation was the introduction of a 'Lilliput' series of 20mm plastic figures. They were particularly short lived, and disappeared quickly from the catalogue. By 1968 Britains' catalogue contained several plastic series all 54mm standard size. Another series which did not last long were the 40mm 'Mini-sets'. The 1970s saw all Britains' figures at the same 1/32 or 54mm scale.

One section of their military toys which are of the very highest quality and quite unique in scope, are the transport and artillery pieces. The horse-drawn gun team was brought out in 1906, wearing collar harness. This was followed shortly by the horse-drawn ambulance (Plate 39), service corps and engineers' waggons, and a

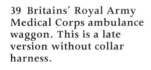

39 Britains' Royal Army Medical Corps ambulance waggon. This is a late version without collar harness.

pontoon section. Just prior to the beginning of the Second World War Britains began to introduce more petrol-driven transport, from two vehicles in 1933 the range rose to 12 by 1940, excluding motorcycles and aeroplanes. The latter catalogue also contained military accessories in the form of army buildings and gun emplacements.

From the very earliest days of production, Britains continued a policy of re-modelling and updating their figures. Pieces brought out in the 1890s were improved during the early years of the 1900s, or before. This process stopped with the passing of the metal figure, plastic ranges were removed and replaced by others usually of a completely different nature.

The first and most noticable alterations were made to horses. Originally the horse was an angular awkward looking beast, having all the jaunty airs of a pony. It was altered to make it a more elegant specimen, with two ears instead of the previous one. The riders also received treatment, they were slimmed down and, if applicable, given a moving arm with cast-on sword. In the case of lancer regiments the cast lance was replaced by a wire one, and the strange cross-legged horse was discontinued. Helmet plumes were made to swing or hang as the figure changed, arms were given different angles, aigulettes appeared and disappeared, as did moustaches. Troopers of the 1st Life Guards can be seen to have been altered at least eight times. The infantry too came in for their share of improvements. Like the cavalrymen they were slimmed down and, anatomically, looked the better for it. Officers foot positions were changed from a 'quarter to three' to 'toe and heel' marching. Full trouser bottoms replaced the 'half booted' or gaitered form. Packs and straps were eventually removed leaving only the waist belt and sashes for officers. Campaign medals disappeared and pigeon chests were smoothed down. Generally these refinements tended to make the figures look better, but removed the odd characterful piece to be found in the early designs.

Britains were fairly economical in the number of different postures they created for infantrymen. These can be summarised for early figures as:

Marching and running, rifles at the slope.
Walking and running, rifles at the trail.
Standing and kneeling to receive cavalry.
Standing, kneeling and lying firing.
On Guard.
Attention.
Present Arms.
Charging.
Later as the nature of warfare changed and more mechanised

transport and artillery were used, the range of postures increased to include specialists in many branches of modern warfare. The casual posture was never to be seen, every Britains' soldier is highly involved in some activity or other, and recent plastic troops continue in this vein of total engagement.

Britains famous red boxes were a stamp of quality and their best known trade mark (Plate 40). The first generation of these long narrow boxes had a printed label with the regimental title and battle honours, surrounded by either a plain or decorative border and Britains' first official trade mark. This was simply 'W. Britain', in script letters, contained within an oblong box. This design developed into a series of very nicely illustrated labels incorporating soldiers, regimental badges, battle honours and the name of the regiment in decorative hand drawn lettering. The whole was surrounded by a drawn border and incorporated Britains' trade mark. The illustrator of these highly individual and now prized labels was Fred Whisstock.

The last form of label to be used on the red-covered boxes was a full-colour item, in contrast to the single printing of the line drawings which preceded it. It portrayed a Scots Greys officer and a Life Guards trumpeter, both dismounted, with the legend 'Britains Soldiers, Regiments of all Nations' between them plus of course Britains' trade mark. The contents were now identified by a small printed label stuck to either end of the box. Latterly Britains packed their soldiers in cellophane-fronted boxes, single figures of the best grade being sold in small illustrated 'picture packs'. The trade mark was supplanted by a more 'up-to-date' job. It comprises a capital 'B' of thick enough proportions to allow a small guardsman to stand in the upright of the letter. Cheaper ranges of figures were contained in brown cardboard boxes with a printed label stuck on top.

Mounted soldiers were originally laid into the box, which had its packing suitably bent to create divisions. This prevented the toys from knocking into each other with consequent damage to paintwork or casting. A much safer method was then devised and they were sewn on to a strip of card which was then stapled on to the bottom of the box. Foot figures were slotted into one edge of the box before they too were sewn in. The numbers of pieces in each box varied depending on the quality and the size. Standard long boxes contained 10 fixed-arm infantry in the early days, changing to eight with the advent of the movable arm. There were usually five mounted pieces to a box. In the smaller 45mm 'B' series there would be six mounted or seven foot.

Britains have always sold composite boxes of soldiers. From the very first year of production (Boxes 4 and 5) carefully selected regiments of infantry, cavalry, artillery, bandsmen and general staff

BRITAINS SOLI

REGIMENTS OF ALL N.

40 Two of Britains' boxes. The upper with an illustrated lid and the figures (Imperial Yeomanry) laid in position, *c.*1900; the lower showing the last design of box lid and the figures (French Cuirassiers) sewn in, *c.*1950.

officers were put together in different combinations and quantities. This series of larger and more expensive items was named 'Displays and Types of the British Army'. The smallest number of pieces was seven and the largest a truly magnificent compendium of their products, containing 274 pieces.

After the Second World War the quantity of metal figures decreased and plastic figures of different historical periods took over. And with this change in the catalogue came a corresponding change in the content of box presentations. Britains at this stage had fewer individual regiments than ever before listed in their catalogues. The accent now was on the production of both protagonists for a particular war or era. Mixed boxes therefore contained either troops of one side or a mixture of both. The smallest box contained the single mounted figure of a Royal Canadian Mounted Policeman, the largest 27 pieces of a British Guards regiment.

One of the criticisms most frequently levelled at Britains' metal toy soldiers is the company's insistence on sticking almost exclusively to representations of contemporary armies. The range of figures outside this sphere included only a few Waterloo, American Civil War and medieval figures. During a period in which the army was active in at least three major wars, it seems fairly obvious that the troops fighting in them would generate most interest. Only recently have they permitted themselves the luxury of casting back and forth in time, and not always with complete success judging by the frequent removals from the catalogue.

The Range of Figures

The foundation of Britains lines of toy soldiers is essentially contained in the first four hundred or so boxes which they marketed. After that, with of course some notable exceptions, it was mainly a case of adding to, and expanding, ranges already started. A selective look at these boxes will give a good impression of the effort they put into what was to become a remarkable achievement.

William Britains' first box of soldiers introduced in 1893 contained an officer and four troopers of the 1st Life Guards (Plate 41). Box 2 was the Royal Horse Guards (the Blues), and 3 was the 5th Dragoon Guards. The same basic casting was used for each regiment, requiring only a different colour of paint to distinguish one from another. They were mounted on the short-lived 'pony' horse with its single ear. Both of the soldiers arms were fixed into position and the right hand had a tin sword cast into it. The boxes contained four troopers on trotting horses and an officer on a prancing horse. Alterations took place to both men and horses and in 1902 the men were fitted with a movable arm.

41 Britains' first figure from Box 1 is shown on the left, 1st Life Guards. Design changes to both horse and man can be seen in the other two examples.

The First Boer War gave Britains the impetus to turn out some Boer Cavalrymen in Box 6. They were dressed in khaki, sported black hats, and had a fixed arm holding either a rifle or a pistol. Infantry did not appear until Box 26 when Boers marching at the slope with oval bases were added. They were changed in 1906 to figures shouldering arms and standing at the ready. These Boer figures did not last long and were discontinued before the start of the First World War.

Britains' first British infantry figures were representatives of the Royal Fusiliers (Plate 42). They were larger than standard and had their hand and rifle plugged into the cuff. This figure was reduced in size and given a movable arm, full equipment and an oval base in 1897. An officer with a fixed arm and a line of medals gave way shortly afterwards to the movable arm and drawn sword version. Boxes 9, 12 and 13 contained the 4th, 11th and 3rd Hussars respectively. Once again the original casting was with a fixed arm, only later in 1909 was it changed to a movable one.

The first highland regiment, the Black Watch, was brought out in 1894 as Box 11. The Argyll & Sutherland Highlanders followed later in the same year as Box 15. These figures, all on oval bases, had their gun hand plugged in at the cuff. The highland sets were issued with a piper. By 1903 the Scottish regiments had been augmented by the addition of Box 77, the Gordon Highlanders; Box 88 the Seaforth Highlanders; and Box 89 the Cameron Highlanders. The original 'running at the trail' types had been changed for a one piece charging figure with fixed bayonet. Still however on the oval stand.

The kilted figures were a popular line always selling well at home

and abroad (Plate 43). Britains continually added to them and used them frequently in composite boxes. The addition of figures in new postures can be easily demonstrated with the highland regiments.

The Black Watch, as well as Box 11 (charging), were given Box 122 (standing firing), Box 2109 (pipe band), Box 2111 (colour party) and Box 2179 (small pipe band). The Argyll's came off badly with the addition only of a six-piece Box 2063. The Gordons in Box 77 were at the slope, in Box 118 they were lying firing, Box 157 (standing, kneeling and lying firing), Box 437 (officers mounted and on foot), Box 1325 another (standing, kneeling and lying firing) and Box 2168 contained the single figure of a mounted officer. Box 88 contained the Seaforths as did Box 112 (slope) and the 17-piece Box 2962. The

42 Britains' Fusiliers and Line Infantry with a nurse and wounded. The first version fusilier is on the extreme left with oval stand and 'quarter to three' feet, next to him is the improved version. The plain coloured infantryman on the left is painted gilt for cheapness.

43 A selection of Britains' Highlanders. Left to right; officer with binoculars on moving arm; standing, kneeling and lying firing both fully coloured and khaki; Waterloo figures, officer, sergeant and private; the Highland Light Infantry; early plug-handed figure on oval base; and a piper of the Royal Scots.

Camerons had Boxes 89 (standing, kneeling and lying firing), 114 (active service order) and the 18-piece Box 2025. Box 2168 contained the mounted Gordons officer and was one of the last pieces Britains made. So the Highland regiments spanned the whole period of production.

Three regiments of line infantry came out in 1894. They were Box 16 the East Kent Regiment, Box 17 the Somerset Light Infantry and Box 18 the Worcestershire Regiment. The figures were standing and kneeling to receive cavalry (Plate 42). Officers originally with fixed arms and medals were improved and given movable arms and swords in 1905. The Band of the Line was Box 27, and the Drums and Bugles of the Line Box 30.

At this stage, in 1895, Britains brought out one of their most attractive sets in Box 28 the Mountain Artillery (Coloured Plate 18). It comprised four mules, each carrying part of a gun and some ammunition, six gunners on foot and a mounted officer. In common with most of the early sets the men had oval bases, which were changed along with the mules and officer's horse some years later.

Boxes 31, 1st Dragoons; 32, 2nd Dragoons (Royal Scots Greys) (Plate 45); and 33, 16th Lancers added to the selection of cavalry (Plates 46, 47, 48). The Grenadier Guards were in Box 34 and the Band of the Coldstream Guards in Box 37. Then came another rather special set in Box 39. The Royal Horse Artillery Gun Team in review order, at the gallop. This set formed the basis for a fine series of gun teams of both the Royal Horse and Royal Field Artillery, in review and active service order.

44 Britains' Soldier to Shoot figure.

45 Some Britains' British cavalry. Left to right; 1st Dragoon Guards; 11th Hussars; Life Guards Farrier; Middlesex Yeomanry dated 1901; 2nd Dragoons (Royal Scots Greys).

46 Britains' early lancers had a cast lance and a 'cross-legged' horse with a single ear.

47 A selection of Britains' British Lancers. Left to right; 16th dated 1903; 5th dated 1903; 12th dated 1903; 12th late version; 17th pre-dating, in the active service dress worn at the Battle of Ulundi.

48 Britains' officer of the 9th Lancers 'turned in the saddle'.

In 1896 Britains began to produce regiments of the Indian Army and Box 45, 3rd Madras Cavalry; Box 46, 10th Bengal Lancers; and Box 47, 1st Bengal Cavalry are examples. Later Boxes 60–68 contained more Indian regiments including infantry, (excluding Box 65 which had a mixture of Russian Cavalry and Infantry). The Royal Navy was not forgotten and Boxes 78, 79 and 80 contained Bluejackets RN, a Naval Landing Party with breach-loading field gun, and White-jackets RN.

It was by popular demand that in 1898 Britains put the 17th Lancers on the market in Box 81. They were wearing the active service dress worn at their famous charge against the Zulus at Ulundi. Also in Box 94 was another famous regiment, the 21st Lancers in the active service dress worn at the Battle of Omdurman.

The Second Boer War saw the introduction of several khaki-clad regiments. In 1900 Box 104 contained the City Imperial Volunteers standing with fixed bayonets (Plate 49). They had an officer, who in

49 Britains' City Imperial Volunteers.

a different shade of paint and in another box, doubled as a Boer. Box 105 were mounted troopers of the Imperial Yeomanry, and with their head changed to one with a foreign service helmet they became Box 108 the 6th Dragoons. The year 1901 brought further Boer War additions. Box 109 contained the Dublin Fusiliers running at the trail and the Devonshire Regiment in Box 110 marching at the slope. Both of these regiments wore the smooth foreign service helmets which were later changed to Wolseley helmets. Box 119 was the Gloucestershire Regiment standing firing.

Another topical army was added to in 1901 – the Egyptians. Their Camel Corps had already appeared in Box 48, but it was not until Box 115 arrived that we had Egyptian Cavalry (lancers and officer). This was immediately followed by Box 116 Sudanese Infantry and Box 117 Egyptian Infantry. The Bikanir Camel Corps of the Indian Army was in Box 123.

Two 45mm 'B' series gun teams were Boxes 125 Royal Horse Artillery in review order and 126 the same in active service order. Box 127 contained the 7th Dragoon Guards and Box 128 the 12th Lancers. Britains then put four of their biggest composite sets into the list. Box 129 contained five regiments making a total of 70 pieces; Box 130 the Scots Guards totalling 118 pieces; Box 131 the biggest ever, containing 274 pieces of infantry and cavalry representing some 15 different regiments; and Box 132, 167 pieces from 14 regiments.

These were truly mammoth productions, and remain unequalled in size and scope of contents by any other manufacturer of toy soldiers.

50 Some of Britains' 'B' series 45mm cavalry. Left to right; Mounted Infantry; 11th Hussars; 16th Lancers; Russian Cossacks; Royal Scots Greys.

51 Britains' motor cycle
machine gun

With one or two exceptions, which will be noted shortly, Britains, from Box 133 up to 197, concentrated their effort on foreign armies. Boxes 133 and 136 contained Russian Infantry and Cavalry (Cossacks) respectively; 134 and 135 Japanese Infantry and Cavalry. The French Army then came in for treatment and Box 138 contained Cuirassiers, Box 139 Chasseurs à cheval, Box 140 Dragoons, Box 141 Infanterie de Ligne and Box 142 Zouaves. Somewhat out of character came Box 147 Charging Zulus. Britains then went on to cover regiments from Prussia; Italy, including Box 169 Bersaglieri; Greece; Serbia and Montenegro. These troops were exclusively in review order, the latter three only being represented by infantry. The Austro-Hungarian Empire had four boxes, 175 Lancers, 176 Dragoons, 177 Infantry of the Line and 178 Foot Guards. They were followed by 186 Mexican Infantry, Belgians, Turcos, 196 Greek Evzones and 197 the Gurkha Rifles.

The exceptions previously mentioned belong to the British Army and were Box 144 Royal Field Artillery; Box 145 the Royal Army Medical Corps; Box 146 the Army Service Corps; Box 159 the Territorial Army; Box 160 Territorials in Khaki. Box 198 contained a Machine Gun Section; Box 199 Motor Cycle Machine Guns (Plate 51); and Box 200 Dispatch Rider on a Motor Cycle.

During this period up to the First World War Britains also made the Salvation Army, Boy Scouts, Arabs, Railway Station Staff etc in standard size.

After the First World War production resumed with Box 201 containing Mounted Officers of the General Staff in befeathered 'fore and aft' hats. The Scottish regiments were rounded off with Box 212 the Royal Scots and Box 213 the Highland Light Infantry. Britains brought out another of their spectacular transport sets in Box 203. It was a horse-drawn Pontoon Section in review order, made up of a four horse team, two of them ridden, pulling a waggon with a wooden pontoon and folding bridge sections perched on top. It was re-issued in active service order some time later as Box 1254.

The Argentinian Republic was then given five boxes; 216 contained Infantry; 217 Cavalry; 219 Military School Cadets; 343 Cavalry and Infantry; and 342 again Cavalry and Infantry. All these were in review order. The Republic of Uruguay followed with three boxes; 220 Cavalry; 221 Military School Cadets and 222 Infantry, all in review order.

After the British Army the nation receiving the greatest attention from Britains was the United States. Before the First World War they had only two boxes ascribed to them, Box 91 United States Infantry and Box 149 American Soldiers. By the 1930s this balance had been redressed, and Britains had 51 sets (including aviators, sailors and marines) in their catalogue. Two sets worthy of mention were Box 226 West Point Cadets in Winter Dress and Box 299 West Point Cadets in Summer Dress. Two other nations appearing in the early 1930s were Box 202 Togoland Warriors, and Box 241 Chinese Infantry in review order.

Between the Boxes in the middle 240s and the first few boxes of the 300s Britains concentrated largely on mixed sets. There was however a small section devoted to American Soldiers, and Box 255 the Green Howards and Box 258 British Infantry in Khaki wearing gas masks.

Guns and gunners have an obvious popularity with the child. They are one of the elements of toy soldiery which not only look imposing when set up, but can be operated with accompanying bangs and flying projectiles. By 1933 Britains catalogue had a rich selection of Horse and Field Artillery teams. In standard size the Royal Horse Artillery was represented by Box 39, review order at the gallop (Plates 52 and 53); Box 1339, active service order at the gallop; and Box 316, review order with the team standing still. The Royal Field Artillery had Box 144 review order at the gallop; Box 1440 active service order at the gallop; and Box 317 review order with the team standing still. Box 318 had a gun, limber and team, the active service order gunners were standing and kneeling. There were also two 'B' series gun teams.

VII (top left) Solid figure of Napoleon by Lucotte of Paris, *c.* 1870. From the collection of the Duke of Marlborough and on show in Blenheim Palace.

VIII (top right) Solid figure of an Hussar by Lucotte of Paris, *c.* 1870. From the collection of the Duke of Marlborough and on show in Blenheim Palace.

IX Solid figure of a Mameluke Drummer by Lucotte of Paris, *c.* 1870. From the collection of the Duke of Marlborough and on show in Blenheim Palace.

52 Britains' Royal Horse Artillery gun team at the gallop. This is a late version with simplified harness.

One or two very attractive sets were numbered in the 300s. Box 312 Grenadier Guards in grey Winter Overcoats; Box 320 Royal Army Medical Corps; Box 321 the Fife and Drum Band of Line Infantry; and Box 322 the same for the Coldstream Guards. Perhaps the most enduring of them all was Box 329 Scots Guards Sentry and Box. Three other boxes which stood the test of time from later additions were Box 400 the Life Guards in Cloaks; Box 429 a mixture of Life and Scots Guards; and Box 432 German Infantry and Officer in active-service dress.

Between the two World Wars Britains' production concentrated largely on increasing the number of postures and activities for the more popular regiments already available. Removing from their list less well known and obsolete pieces, and adding more khaki-clad troops of Great Britain (Plate 54) and the United States. There was also

a rapid increase in petrol driven transport. The Carden Loyd Tank
was no longer alone on the list. Boxes 1334 and 1335 contained four
and six wheeled lorries; Box 1448 an Army Staff Car; Box 1876 a
Bren Gun Carrier and Crew; and Box 1877 a Beetle Lorry. A monstrous
Heavy Duty Lorry on 18 rubber-tyred wheels in Box 1641 could be
used to transport guns and searchlights, as in Boxes 1642 and 1643
respectively. There were also a fine series of anti-aircraft defence
services, Searchlights, Predictors, Height Finders and Sound
Locators all with operators.

Britains in later years experimented with changes in period. The
first was Box 1258 Knights; this was followed by Boxes 1516 and 1518
(Waterloo) Infantry; and Boxes 1517 and 1519 (Waterloo) Highlanders.
They reverted once again to the middle ages and produced six boxes
of knights, 1659–64 and another in the late 1950s, numbered 2161.
The American Civil War had nine boxes of cavalry, infantry and
artillery devoted to it, 2055–60 and 2068–70.

The company reached a peak in soldier design and production with one figure from a sporadic series depicting the Fort Henry Guards of Canada. There had been several boxes brought out when finally Box 2182 containing the Fort Henry Guard Pioneer made its appearance. This bearded figure with full equipment, spade, white apron and his hands resting on an axe is an absolutely magnificent creation, and one of Britains' last.

The year 1960 was a turning point in Britains' history, apart from heralding the end of metal figures, the company brought out their own plastics made in Britain.

Other British Makers

Until the beginning of the twentieth century, Britains had no home-based rivals to compete with in the manufacture of toy soldiers. Their great success encouraged others to make efforts to emulate them, and between 1900 and 1914 eight competitors started up. Their names were: C D Abel; BMC; A Fry Ltd (Plate 56); Hanks Bros & Co. Ltd; John Hill & Co; Reka (C W Baker); James S Renvoize; and the Russell Manufacturing Co Ltd.

54 Some Britains' khaki figures. Left to right; WWII British Infantry; Royal Artillery gunners with gun; United Nations soldier with slung rifle; WWI soldier wearing a gas mask; WWI machine gunner.

Like Britains they were London based, and their products were mainly hollow-casts. With some exceptions they made their pieces to approximately the 54mm standard size. The quality of their collective products varied enormously, the best, which was not a lot, were very good, much of the rest were of a low standard. Occasionally an inspired figure would make its appearance, but Britains high and

55 Britains' British ski trooper.

constant quality was never really challenged. There was a similarity in the choice of ranges these firms produced. Most frequent were British Line Infantry in scarlet jacket and spiked helmet; khaki-clad infantry with flat caps and puttees; and regiments of foot and horse guards in ceremonial dress; and of course the kilted Highland regiments. Nurses of the Royal Army Medical Corps received a lot of attention, and they can usually be numbered amongst the best pieces from each maker.

Of specific manufacturers BMC's catalogue boasted all the regiments of the British regular army, along with representatives from Australia, Belgium, France, Germany, India, Italy, Russia, and a few Zulus. It was however the firm of John Hill & Co., founded in 1900 by a Mr Wood, that took the position of being 'second to Britains' both in size and quality of output. The scope of Hill's catalogue too was impressive. It is unfortunate that owing to the constant production and speedy cessation of figures, as world events changed, it is

56 Wind-up tin soldier made before 1916. 145mm.

not possible to compile an accurate list of the firm's products. The casting and painting of soldiers was always good, but there is a distinct disparity between the design quality of foot figures and their skinny mounted colleagues (Plates 57 and 58).

As with all their contemporaries the foundation of Hill's range was laid firmly on regiments of the British Army. Infantry of the Line were available standing at the ready; standing and kneeling firing; marching at the slope; and running at the trail. This latter figure had the advantage of a movable arm, more usually associated with Britains. Early pieces had oval bases and 'half boots' or gaiters. The first editions of khaki clad infantrymen had flat caps and puttees. They came in the usual varieties; ordered arms; marching at the slope; charging; firing; throwing stick bombs; standing and kneeling machine gunners; a drummer and his very tall companion bugler. Hill's then made steel-helmeted Second World War figures when the gas mask made its appearance.

The Second World War gave greater scope to Hills for their range of khaki troops. They contributed some very interesting figures such as the soldier in gas mask, anti-gas cape and trousers with a detector cloth on his fixed bayonet; or the British Infantryman at the slope with a ring instead of a hand, into which could be fitted a rifle, bren

57 Hollow-cast figures by Fry.

58 Hollow-casts by John Hill & Co. Left to right; WWI British Infantry; WWI French Infantry with colours; British Lancer; British Hussar; American Civil War soldier and officer.

gun or pick axe. Medical units were obtainable in both active service dress and review order, comprising stretcher parties, doctors and nurses. Their series of anti-aircraft defence services were poorly represented in comparison to Britains, with only a Height Finder and Operator and an Observer in a Spotting Chair. The Royal Flying Corps, Royal Air Force and the Women's Auxiliary Air Force ranges contained some very good figures. Notably the RFC pilot walking along pulling on his gloves, and the RAF pilots running in full flying kit.

The guards were in full dress but could also be obtained in greatcoats. They had a band, colour bearer and officers. Highland regiments marched, shot, charged and stood, all to the accompaniment of a pipe band. Although they were generally kilted, one soldier was made in trews. Of the few territorial regiments reaching makers catalogues, the London Scottish predominated. Hill's figure was kneeling firing.

British cavalry regiments were present in the form of Life Guards and Royal Horse Guards, both with fixed and movable arms; Life Guards in cloaks with movable arms; Lancers and Hussars with movable arms; the Royal Scots Greys with a trumpeter and standard bearer; and khaki cavalry wearing either steel helmets or peaked caps. They were rounded off by a fixed arm Field Marshal.

Soldiers of other nations were not well represented in Hill's catalogue. The United States of America has most, and is fairly well represented in khaki from both world wars. There are also West Point Cadets, Marines and the 42nd Regiment of New York. Soldiers

103

of the Union and Confederacy during the American Civil War are
there in force. They were cast in many firing positions, also charging,
marching and with cavalry. Of other countries only the armies of
Abyssinia, Austro-Hungaria, Ethiopia, France, Finland, Greece,
India, Italy, Japan and Turkey are present, although one might add
the Royal Canadian Mounted Police and Zulus.

Apart from the purely military models the company had a long
list of civilian and popular subjects which included; Lifeboatmen;
Farriers; Zoo and Farm Animals; Knights; Romans; Spacemen;
Railway Staff and Passengers; Police; and Indians and Cowboys.

The end of the First World War saw six of the early firms give up
trading, only John Hill & Co and Reka were left. Between the two
world wars three more filled the gaps. Charbens & Co Ltd founded
by the Reid brothers, the Crescent Toy Co Ltd and Taylor and Barrett

60 Hollow-cast Life Guard sentry and box by Crescent.

all started in London. Of them Crescent were the biggest and had the most extensive catalogue (Plate 60). A very amusing piece which came from them was a rickshaw being pulled by a little Chinaman with a lady passenger and child riding in it.

During and immediately after the Second World War three more firms joined the list. Two of them Cherilea Products and Fylde & Co (Plate 61) started in Blackpool; Cherilea incorporated Fylde in 1950. The third of the trio, Timpo, grew to become one of the largest manufacturers, changing their name in 1953 to Model Toys Ltd.

Timpo's figures on the whole are of a high standard, the best of them compare well with the best of Britains (Plate 62). Their output covered the usual ground and included guards, Life Guards, Highlanders, khaki infantry, West Point Cadets and Cowboys and Indians. One range which is absolutely outstanding is their portrayal

105

of the American Army during the Second World War. The figures are superbly designed, well made and painted. Among those available in steel helmets were soldiers kneeling on one knee holding a mug and eating; doing their washing in a bucket; reading a map; operating a field telephone; walking with a slung rifle and full equipment; at ease; standing, kneeling and lying firing; charging; crawling; throwing grenades; using mine detectors; firing bazookas; machine gunners; military police; carrying a stretcher; firing a mortar; officers with binoculars and pistols; and a motor cycle dispatch rider. Some including an officer and standard bearer were wearing forage caps, and many were available painted as caucasians or negroes.

Sets of medieval knights based on films, farm animals, circus, railway figures, police, arctic explorers, dogs and others came from this firm.

Other companies during the course of these years came and went. Names like Stoddart Ltd, Benbros, Roydon, Sacall and Astra-Pharos

61 Hollow-cast Dragoon and Beefeater by Fylde.

62 Hollow-casts by Timpo. Left to right; WWII British Infantry; WWII American Mortar Team; American West Point Cadet bandsmen.

each left a small contribution to enrich the records. The larger and more successful companies moved from metal to plastic and survived, their catalogues now however display few toy soldiers.

The process of hollow-casting toy soldiers was a British innovation. It was used for a short time in Germany, not so much as a medium for creative modelling, more as a method of lightening heavy pieces for export. Complete German hollow-cast figures are not of high standard and are considered in Germany to be very much second rate.

America did not take to the home produced hollow-cast either. This is not surprising as imported Britains figures were easily obtainable, their standard was high and their cost low. The background to American production, as far as it went, is difficult to piece together. Looked at broadly there is no evidence at all that commercially made mass-produced metal toy soldiers were made until the early years of this century. Two companies, the American Soldier Company and McLoughlin Brothers, both of New York, made some efforts at hollow-casting. The designs bear a strong resemblance to Britains, but the results were not at all notable. Others followed, and from time to time one finds an oddity of American origin but with little hope of identifying it.

The United States has no tradition of hollow-cast toy soldiers and collections are based on Britains, or French and German solids.

Identification

The hollow-cast is very light in relation to its size, and a sharp tap will give off a hollow ring. Close examination will disclose a tiny hole in the casting, this is generally to be found on the head of both men and horses. Mounted figures can be either cast on to their horses or separate. The horses do not have stands (except for the very rare rear-legged stand cavalry officers), and apart from Britains curious 'cross-legged' lancer the figures and horses are fully three dimensional.

In common with all other types of toy soldiers we have looked at, many hollow-casts have no marks of identification on them. Fortunately, however, most of the sales literature and catalogues are still to be found. It is therefore not difficult in most cases to name the maker and approximately the date of manufacture. Also it was found possible to obtain some degree of design protection under the Sculpture Copyright Act of 1814. One of the conditions was that the makers name had to be on each casting. So the majority of manufacturers creating original designs cast some mark of identification on their pieces. Some of the hard-to-identify figures come from the moulds of pirates who blatantly copied and sold other people's figures.

The markings of the main manufacturers were as follows:

William Britains
Britains' markings were started in 1900 and are confined to the underside of infantry stands and horse's bellies. The first ones on infantry stands were small paper discs which were used until 1905. The first regiment so dated was the City Imperial Volunteers.

1900–12	COPYRIGHT Wm BRITAINS JR with the addition of the date of manufacture and occasionally MADE IN ENGLAND
1913	BRITAINS LTD. COPYRIGHT. PROPRIETORS
1924–37	BRITAINS LTD. COPYRIGHT. PROPRIETORS MADE IN ENGLAND
1938–46	COPYRIGHT BRITAINS LTD MADE IN ENGLAND
1947–56	BRITAINS LTD ENGLAND

The French office which opened in 1905 followed the British pattern of markings with the addition DEPOSÉ and the date of introduction to France. In 1913 it changed to exactly the British pattern and in 1919 it added DEPOSÉ once again.

Charbens & Co Ltd
CHARBENS MADE IN ENGLAND or C & CO LTD

Cherilea
CHERILEA MADE IN ENGLAND

Crescent Toy Co Ltd
MADE IN ENGLAND

A Fry Ltd
A FRY LTD LONDON sometimes with an added date

Hanks Bros & Co Ltd
H HANKS COPYRIGHT

John Hill & Co
JOHN HILL or J. HILLCO or JO HILL or JOHILLCO or ENGLAND
Unlike Britains, Hills did not confine their marks to any specific position. They will be found under the base and on the figure itself.

Reka
REKA COPYRIGHT or REKA COPYRIGHT C W BAKER MADE IN ENGLAND

James S Renvoize
J RENVOIZE COPYRIGHT and the date

Russell Manufacturing Co Ltd
RUSSELL MFG CO LTD occasionally with a number and date

Taylor & Barrett
T & B COPYRIGHT ENGLAND

Timpo
TIMPO TOYS ENGLAND

7 Toy Soldiers Today

The Decline in Production

During the years of the two World Wars toy soldiers took a back seat in the priorities of metal usage and production time. The companies making them either stopped and closed down, or went over to the manufacture of munitions and other war supplies. After the wars there was a general shortage of metal, and the little that was available for such luxuries as toys was largely earmarked for export. Makers' ranges were, of necessity, curtailed.

There was, in addition, a stronger feeling of national revulsion to warfare than had been the case with small remote colonial conflicts. The numbers of troops engaged had risen dramatically and casualty lists were long. Few families escaped totally unscathed. Civilian populations were no longer onlookers; at a time of war they were now active participants. Widespread heavy bombing brought into the home the harsh reality previously confined to remote battlefields.

These experiences coupled with the drab khaki of the active-service uniforms that were now exclusively used, took much of the popular glamour out of soldiering. So the toy soldier had to suffer and its numbers inevitably dwindled. These were the years when the toy firms found greater sales for their non-military lines. Interest shifted on to the model farm and zoo, the hunt and circus. Toy cars and toy trains had a consumer boom and evolved, with the metal toy soldier, into carefully detailed and produced scale models. Labour difficulties also intervened and the expert craftsmen who cast toy soldiers, and the outworkers who painted them were no longer available.

63 Plastic figures. Left to right; Starlux German officer, 65mm; Elastolin knight, 52mm; Elastolin Roman, 104mm; Mokarex French Infantry, 65mm; Marx British Infantry, 130mm; Russian Infantry, 54mm (made in Russia, maker unknown); Segom French Infantry, 56mm.

In 1967 the British Government introduced new regulations to control the safety of toys made and sold in Britain. These, amongst other things, influenced the substance of toys manufactured and the ingredients of the paint they were coated with. Traditional toy soldiers unfortunately had a high lead content on both counts. As lead imbibed or handled in sufficient quantities can be injurious to health, it helped to end the days of the metal soldier as a toy. Quite perceptibly in the late 1950s and very early 1960s they quietly slid out of the catalogues. A small quantity were made exclusively for the export market but they too dried up and disappeared. The hollow-cast metal soldier had become a thing of the past. It acquired a new status and a new set of values as soon as production ceased.

From the earliest days of the mass-produced toy soldier, manu-facturers had searched for a cheaper and more easily obtainable production substance. The answer was already edging on to the market in household and scientific lines – plastic. Plastic had been used for making toy soldiers as early as 1945, although it did not meet with immediate approval it would not be long before it usurped metal as the main ingredient for a successful and inexpensive toy.

Plastic as a toy-making material has inexorably forged ahead since its introduction. In the world of toy soldiers, plastics during the 30 or so years of their existence, have received only lukewarm interest from collectors whose buying and collecting desires give a basically cheap object greater value.

Plastic Soldiers

The word plastic (Greek *plastikos*) means quite simply a substance which is both malleable and capable of being moulded. This des-cription is equally applicable to substances as diverse as metal and clay. Common usage has narrowed this definition and it could be generally said that plastics are recognised as emanating from the three main groupings of polyvinylchlorides, polyethylenes and polystyrenes. So what are correctly termed plastic toy soldiers are produced from materials covered by one of these headings. Each has a set of distinctive chemical properties giving different physical aspects to the finished product. Two of the most important for toy manufacturers to consider are those governing the capacity of the material to accept paint and be glued or solvent welded.

Most of the early commercially successful plastic toy soldiers were simple one-piece castings. As working knowledge of plastic materials expanded the capacity to control and use them grew. Consumer acceptance, although slow at first, was gained and the makers became more adventurous in their efforts. Soon complex multi-piece toy soldiers became commonplace. They were capable of being more interesting in posture and could be made in great numbers.

Manufacturers all over the world turned to this inexpensive new material. Most countries now have a plastic toy soldier industry with the result that the market is flooded with their products. They can be bought singly or in sets; jumbled in plastic bags; carefully slotted into boxes; or not even removed from the casting sprue.

Many of the longer established toy soldier producers utilised their old metal moulds for plastic casting. Some individuals and companies approached the problem of plastics more creatively and designed especially for the medium. A flexible moulding material and the ease of solvent welding or plugging, has allowed a lot more freedom in the animation of figures. Designers are now able to create soldiers in a variety of action and casual poses never before possible.

The comparative simplicity of the injection moulding process over metal casting has unfortunately meant that unscrupulous people are able more easily to pirate figures. This is now happening more than ever and their wares are frequently to be found in plastic bags imported from the Far East.

Toy soldier quality and design fluctuates from maker to maker. The best as usual are exceptionally good, but the worst achieve a level of banality never reached in metal. The ability of plastic to show detail more clearly and mould better undercuts has often been ignored to the ultimate detriment of figures. Often the fact that plastic is being used appears to be adequate excuse for a substantial drop in standard.

They have an inherent greasiness and flexibility, which coupled with a resistance to paint adhesion does not help endear them to collectors. It is little wonder that plastic soldiers have a lean time on the antique soldier market.

Fulfilling their prime purpose as children's toys, plastic soldiers have advantages over metal. They can be safely chewed, sucked or fingered without danger to health, and their cost means that a large army is within most young pockets.

Some Prominent Makers

From a creative standpoint the French and Germans have an outstanding record in the field of plastic toy soldiers (Plate 63). Prominent among the early makers is the French firm of Starlux. They started in 1900 with a composition substance similar to Elastolin, going over to plastic in 1945. Their toughened polystyrene gives a good hard-finished product. It paints and welds easily as can be seen from their well animated and carefully painted soldiers.

Starlux have a constantly expanding range embracing mainly Napoleonic and modern troops. All the mounted Napoleonics are worthy of mention, along with the band of the Foot Grenadiers of the Imperial Guard, French Foreign Legion and Second World War Germans. Their figures come in two sizes, a large collectors size at 70mm and a wargame size at 30mm.

Another French firm that of Segom (Société d'Édition Générale d'Objects Moulés) using a similar polystyrene produces figures from the most popularly modelled periods in French history, the Revolution and the First Empire. Characterised by an incredibly pompous elegance, these soldiers are an absolute joy to look at. Painting is simple but accurate, complementing exactly the animation. They can be obtained as unpainted castings for assembly or as ready constructed and painted figures.

In Germany the premier firm is without doubt O & M Hausser's Elastolin. With a magnificent tradition of toy soldier making already behind them they started moving to polystyrene in 1958. Modern soldiers, except for the Swiss, no longer have a place in their catalogue. The available range now includes; Romans; Vikings; Huns; Normans; Landsknechts; eighteenth century Prussian Infantry; American War of Independence; and Cowboys and Indians. These are enhanced by a series of siege equipment, guns and castles. Animals figure prominently and have not been better made by any other manufacturer. Soldiers are made in two sizes, 70 and 40mm. Most riders are detachable from their horses, the standard of painting is high and animation could not be bettered.

The figures from these three companies are at the very expensive end of the toy soldier market. They are quite simply the best available.

Other European makers whose pieces reach a commendably high standard are the coffee firm of Mokarex in France. Their creations, of standard size, are cast in a bronze or silver coloured single piece unit. They are characterised by good modelling and careful attention to national facial characteristics. Walter Merten in Germany with his Berliner figures; Café Storme in Belgium (another coffee firm); and Reamsa in Spain all produce highly individual soldiers.

An interesting point about European manufacturers is that most of them have chosen to use a toughened polystyrene, which is capable of great versatility and sharpness of detail.

British interest in plastic soldiers goes back, like the French, to the early pioneering days. Just after the Second World War a Polish gentleman named Mr Zang produced a range of figures which he marketed under the name 'A Zang Product'. His designer and partner was Roy Selwyn-Smith. The name of his range was soon changed to 'Herald'. Figure design was exceptionally good and a plasticised polyvinylchloride chosen to cast from. Predictably the range followed the popular pattern and consisted of foot guards, horse guards, Highlanders with a pipe band, cowboys and indians, and WWII British Infantry in action. Unusual early pieces were Indian Army infantry; Robin Hood; and a series of dancers. Later extensions came in the form of Trojans, knights in armour; and more recently the 7th Cavalry and a Roman chariot. These are all standard size and with the exception of the Indian Army, Robin Hood and the dancers are all still available. A comparison between the earlier cowboys and Trojans,

64 Plastic figures. Left to right; Herald WWII British Infantry; Britains' Deetail WWII American Infantry; Starlux 30mm French Officer; Britains' Swoppet Mortar Team; Airfix 20mm WWI British Wiring Party; Britains' Eyes Right Royal Marine bandsman; Airfix WWII German soldier.

and more recent additions show that the design standard is perhaps not being maintained.

In 1953 Mr Zang's Herald enterprise was taken over by the Britains company of metal fame. Herald models, made in Hong Kong, were advertised as a section of the Britains range (Plate 64).

Britains began their own plastic venture with a set in 1957 named 'Lilliput'. It consisted of a shallow box with circular windows containing eight 20mm British Second World War infantry figures, they were very good scaled-down versions of the Herald range. This was later followed by 'Eyes Right', made of a similar material to Herald, and fully up to the high standard of the disappearing metal lines. Britains 1968 catalogue lists the two sides of the American Civil War, infantry, cavalry and artillery; Life Guards, Life Guards escorting the sovereign's standard, a mounted band of the Life Guards, Horse Guards, Scots Guards with Colours and Band, Royal Marines with Band, Middlesex Regiment with Drums and Bugles, United States Marine Corps with Colours and Band, and the Royal Canadian Mounted Police. A range of 'Swoppets' is also there. It included American War of Independence infantry, British WWII infantry, knights, cowboys and indians. A typical Swoppet would be constructed from seven or eight separate parts which could be detatched and interchanged to allow for variety.

The 1970s saw the end of the Eyes Right series, except for the Mounties, and the Swoppets. Both were overtaken by 'Deetail', a new series with metal bases. The 1974 catalogue shows American Civil War, WWII British, German, Japanese, and United States

115

infantry, cowboys and indians, knights and Turks, British and French Waterloo infantry and cavalry. With the exception of the latter set, which does not achieve the highest standards of design, the Deetail series is excellent. Strangely enough one is able to accept a prong from the stand poking into a horse's belly to hold it up, but soft plastic bendy guns and swords are still rather incongruous.

Airfix Products Ltd are the other major British toy soldier manufacturers. Using a polyethylene for figures and polystyrene for buildings and vehicles, they have one of the widest ranges of military toys available. There are two scales for figures, 54mm standard and 20mm wargame. In the larger size there are currently 14 sets, 4 from the Waterloo period containing British and French infantry, and 10 from WWII of German, British, American, Russian, Japanese and Australian infantry. These are all one piece figures of exceptionally high quality both in casting and design.

Forty-four different boxes of 20mm figures are listed in the 1974 catalogue. A unique contribution to the world of plastic toy soldiers, it covers Waterloo, First World War, Second World War, American Civil War, American War of Independence, Wild West, Robin Hood, Romans and Civilians amongst others. Each box has a companion box of protagonists, and they also have military vehicles, gun emplacements, buildings and bridges. Although some of the earlier figures are a little featureless, the latest designed by John Niblett are of very high quality.

From the mid 1950s Britain has had many manufacturers whose products have added to, and still add to, the wide selection available on the market. Prominent are Timpo, Crescent, Lone Star, Johillco, Cherilea and Charbens. In the main, manufacturers brought out knights in armour; Second World War British and American troops; foot and horse guards; and the inevitable cowboys and indians.

In direct contrast to European practice the British use a soft plastic. It has a higher impact strength than the hard plastics, important in the well-filled toy box.

American plastic soldiers are solidly in the able hands of Louis Marx & Co of New York. Their catalogue covers most of the conflicts that American troops were involved in, together with a healthy selection of Western figures complete with buildings and natural elements. Britain is represented by Second World War infantry, some personality figures and a Robin Hood set. Marx manufacture in Britain and America, figures are one-piece castings and the general standard is high.

Many of the connoisseur kits of model soldiers are produced from plastics, the foremost coming from Historex, Almark and more recently Airfix.

65 Some new figure styles coming on to the market. Left to right; 15th Ludhiana Sikhs and Hong Kong Submarine Engineers by Janet Scruby; Life Guard, Scots Guard and Beefeater from Britains' new metal range.

Identification

In the field of toy soldiers plastic, as distinct from metal, wood or composition, is easy to identify. The main features are its light weight in relation to size, even in hard plastics its pliability, and its warmth to the touch. Most plastic soldiers are fully three dimensional or almost so. Although experiments in plastic flats have been made they have never emerged as a commercial entity.

Plastics as already stated are pirated in great numbers and left unmarked. This along with many manufacturers' continued hesitation to mark their products leaves many plastics in the common position of being unidentifiable. Most of the makers mentioned in the text will have their names or trade marks cast clearly on the underside of the base.

The Present Situation

The last few years have seen an upsurge of interest in the wargaming hobby. Modelling magazines carry advertisements from literally dozens of manufacturers of figures from 5 to 35mm. These are mostly metal productions. It would appear that much youthful interest in the subject has moved off the cumbersome 54mm size and on to these tiny inexpensive ones. Battles can be fought quite adequately in a few

117

square feet. Postures and periods are more numerous, and an army can be easily carried in a small box.

Of the major manufacturers only Britains are moving towards metal toys again. Even they have plastic accoutrements and headgear (Plate 65). Manufactured from a light alloy the figures are solid and well designed. A very tourist orientated set it consists in the 1974 catalogue of a Scots Guardsman, a Beefeater and a dismounted Life Guard. Shamus Wade, one of the foremost dealers of old toy soldiers in Britain, has an increasing range of 'Nostalgia Models' in his list. Sculpted by Janet Scruby and painted in the style of the old toy soldier they are amazingly good and reasonably priced. A company in Hong Kong is exporting a metal series which includes Napoleonics, Vikings and Pirates.

Otherwise metal toy soldiers still come from the previously mentioned firms of Wollner (distributed by Josef Kober) in Vienna, Babette Schweizer in Germany and CBG Mignot in France.

8 Building Your Own Collection

Themes

The urge to collect interesting, valuable and beautiful objects has been displayed by mankind for a considerable part of our known history. Until recent times these objects have generally possessed an innate value by virtue of the material of their creation or the craftsmanship in their making. It is an idea born of this century that common everyday objects, buildings and even machinery, which have had an influence on the growth and structure of our society are also worth treasuring. Concern for the preservation of relics of the recent past has reached massive proportions and the cult of collecting them is more widespread than ever.

One important aspect in the life of almost all communities has been of a military nature. This is reflected in the numbers of people involved in hobbies derived from warfare in one or other of its guises. The exact choice of items acquired from this extensive field is usually bounded by the expression of a particular interest or considerations of cost, or both.

It would appear from the comments of collectors that no two collections of basically similar material were ever built up for exactly the same reasons. Consequently the content of collections varies enormously from one to another. So if a collection is being contemplated from the start, or extended, a complex mixture of interests in the army, a regiment, military history, toys etc will provide the reasons for the selection process. A first this could well be entirely subconscious and the shape of the collection formed instinctively.

Like other toys with a very long pedigree the toy soldier has become the object of much attention. In many countries they are collected by individuals, museums or societies, and much time and energy is devoted to the study of this fascinating and absorbing offshoot of military life. Each country has a peculiarly national flavour in the type of toy soldiers preferred, generally founded on the product they themselves have manufactured and are most familiar with.

Germans have a distinct liking for the modern flat. Quite often this will be paraded with thousands of its fellows in a diorama. These form an attractive miniature setting for recording important events. High-quality solids by such masters as Haffner and Heyde take second place, being slow to achieve recognition. In France and most other European countries the solid figure takes precedence followed closely by hollow-casts. Flats and paper sheets come in as a poor third. The British and Americans share an equal interest in hollow-casts and solids, pushing flats once more into third place. Dioramas are more popular in America than in Britain which has never taken to the mass display.

There is a distinctly shady area between toy and model soldiers where poorly made models might be taken as toys, and well-made toys as models. It is only possible to differentiate between them by asking the question 'were they made for a child to play with?' Even the answer to that might not be a definite yes or no. Frequently therefore the collector of toy soldiers is also a collector of model soldiers or vice versa, intentionally or otherwise.

A collector of purely toy soldiers as opposed to a collector of model soldiers has a somewhat different set of parameters to his hobby. Firstly the toy soldier should be retained in as near original condition as possible i.e. the condition in which it left the factory. The collector is not concerned with their re-painting, re-animating, or use as part of a diorama which might involve defacing even the stand. Model soldiers on the other hand are used in exactly the opposite way, i.e. painting, animating and obliterating the stand in a diorama. Secondly toy soldiers are normally to be obtained in four standard variants: officer, soldier, colour bearer and musician. Regimental distinctions between similarly uniformed units often do not show. Model soldiers can be bought in all ranks, most states of uniform regulation, and it is vitally important to be able to distinguish individual units.

These basic differences mean that the collector of toy soldiers uses collecting themes at variance with those of the model soldier collector, although some could be used for either.

1 THE MAKERS

Collecting the pieces of one or more specific makers and perhaps attempting to put their whole range together.

2 BASIC CATEGORIES OF TOY SOLDIERS

Selecting one of the basic categories, i.e. paper, flats, semi-solids, solids, hollow-casts or composition, and building a collection round that.

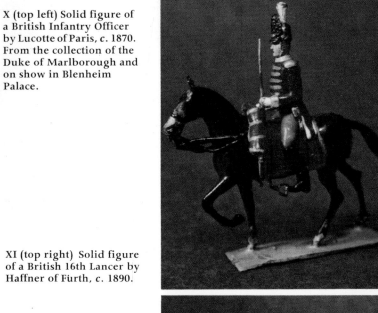

X (top left) Solid figure of a British Infantry Officer by Lucotte of Paris, *c.* 1870. From the collection of the Duke of Marlborough and on show in Blenheim Palace.

XI (top right) Solid figure of a British 16th Lancer by Haffner of Fürth, *c.* 1890.

XII (middle) Group of solid British Infantry by Heyde of Dresden, *c.* 1880.

XIII (bottom) Wooden toy soldiers. Left to right; three British late Victorian pieces; two mid eighteenth century pieces probably German.

3 PERIOD OR WAR

Deciding on a period such as medieval or a specific war like the Second World War and collecting pertinent pieces from any manufacturer, whatever their basic category.

4 COUNTRY

All the pieces which represent regiments from one particular country of interest, incorporating all services and all makers and basic categories.

5 GENERAL HISTORY

Accumulating a collection representative of as many categories, manufacturers and occasional oddities as possible from, perhaps, 1800–1960.

Each of these specimen themes would allow for a collection of some thousands of soldiers to be built up. There is of course no reason why two or more of them should not be combined, or indeed why one's collection should not be an accumulation of the pieces which give most pleasure.

Whatever theme is eventually chosen to guide a collection, the full enjoyment of being a collector is not found simply in the accumulation of hordes of little metal men. Real depth of interest is gained by research and the acquisition of knowledge about the subject; by attempting as complete an identification as possible and by being able to place a figure in its correct position in the chronology of toy-soldier production. Who made the figure? when was it made? has the basic casting been used for any others in the range? has the figure been altered and re-issued? was the mould bought and the piece marketed by some else? is the piece a pirate from the original and what of the company that made it?

Further interest is provided by research into the actual military events which prompted the manufacturers to make the pieces. Or the drawings and paintings of contemporary artists whose work often influenced the design and posture. These endeavours, interesting in themselves, will give a collection greater meaning and the collector a rewarding and absorbing involvement. Widening the scope of interest round these toys enables them to be put into a social and historic context, greatly increasing the joy and delight of ownership.

What to Look for, What to Avoid

Collecting toy soldiers will inevitably lead to the frequent expenditure of money. Naturally it must be parted with wisely and with either good advice or confidence that the figures bought are worth the cost.

The junk shop bargains of a few years ago are becoming rarer as old toys rise in value. There is an unfortunate tendency amongst the owners of such establishments, and of 'antique shops', to believe that any old toy has immense value. This is not so, some because of their age or scarcity command a high price, others sell for little more than their original cost. Often there are repainted, pirated and converted pieces. These can easily trap the inexperienced collector. It is therefore advisable that the beginner buys only from reputable toy soldier dealers until knowledge aids his judgement to do otherwise.

There is no substitute for buying the best toy soldiers available. Well-preserved paintwork on an unbroken casting is the collectors target. Not only does this give the best visual appearance but it retains a greater monetary value. Having made that statement it must be borne in mind that many pieces will be as much as 200 years old. Condition and age must be carefully balanced against each other, along with importance to the collection as a whole.

The following information gives some special points to note, and an idea of general availability for each basic category of toy soldiers.

FLATS

Although large quantities of flat toy soldiers were imported into this country, their fragility and play purpose means that relatively few have survived. There is only sporadic availability and it is necessary to visit dealers, attend auction sales, and generally keep one's eyes open to have a chance of finding them. The cost is reasonable when one considers their age, and a pound or two will buy some fine examples. Camp or bivouac scenes, gun teams and bands are particularly attractive.

SEMI-SOLIDS

Semi-solids are more easily obtained than flats and frequently can be found in antique shops and military dealers, perhaps because they were cheaper and less easily destroyed. Also many of them were home-made between the world wars, and although interesting from this point of view they are of little value. Mainly characterised by poor casting, an absence of detail, and desperately bad painting they are easy to spot.

Good commercially made German semi-solids compare in quality with figures from any of the other categories. Groups of any kind or figures in original boxes are most desirable. Broadly speaking only specimens in good to excellent condition are worth having.

SOLIDS

Solids along with hollow-casts are one of the two most sought-after categories. Dealers will always be able to offer a selection of single pieces and small groups. Figures by Haffner and Lucotte are expensive if you can find them. Heyde and Mignot are more common and a lot less expensive. Once again scenic groups, gun teams, horse-drawn ambulances and figures in their original boxes are much sought after and command a proportionately higher price.

Solids should be examined carefully and if possible compared with others of their kind to check for repainting and touching up. Unless it is felt that a badly scratched or chipped figure is especially significant to the collection, it is better to wait for a better one to turn up.

COMPOSITION

Composition figures should only be bought if they are in pretty good physical shape. Too many are found broken and split with the rusting wire armature showing. These need quick and careful attention if they are not to deteriorate further.

The two principal makers, Elastolin and Lineol, are both fairly well represented on most dealers shelves. Complete sets, attractive groupings, transport and artillery units will command a higher price than single pieces. One group in particular is the personality range of German war leaders.

Figures from these two companies can be quite expensive and are often found to top the cost of good solids and hollow-casts.

WOOD

Wooden toy soldiers are not at all easy to find. If they appeal and the woodworm is not too far advanced, buy them.

HOLLOW-CASTS

Because of the immense quantities produced and production having stopped only recently, hollow-casts are the most common type of toy soldiers offered for sale.

It is possible to buy most of them in a very good state of preservation and this should always be the collector's aim. The condition of the metal casting is all important, and while slight damage to the paintwork can be easily dealt with a broken casting is not so simply and invisibly repaired. Close examination of paintwork and comparison with other similar pieces will show whether a figure has been altered, i.e. repaired, repainted or detailed. None of these conditions are at all desirable, the figure is not in its original state. Its value both as an old toy and financially must suffer.

Figures in their original boxes, preferably still sewn in, gun teams and other pieces of wheeled transport, complete bands on horse or foot are all prized objects. Condition is the main consideration for buying. One can expect to pay more for Britains' productions, followed by Johillco, Timpo and then the other makers.

PLASTICS

In general plastic toy soldiers are easy to obtain in most toy shops and large stores. The earlier pieces, now discontinued, pose a problem. Not having much financial value it is most unusual to find a dealer with any stock of them. Probably in years to come interest in them as collectors items will increase, but while many are still available in shops this will be some years off.

It is a matter of personal choice, availability and cost whether single figures or groups are bought for display. In general the smaller flats and semi-solids look better as a group while larger figures can stand more happily on their own. The matter will probably be solved by buying greater numbers of the pieces which most appeal, and singles of others whose object is only to make up a list or range. A mixture of this sort is more attractive to look at than a stiffly organised definite number of each.

9 Looking After Your Collection

Conservation and Restoration

Antiquities of any description must not be merely cared for, but cared for properly if they are not to deteriorate over a period of time. Consideration given to the physical state of their display and storage will be repayed with a longer life in pristine original condition.

The role of conservation is to prevent the deterioration of any material or to counteract deterioration which has already started, thereby prolonging the life of that material. Conservation is also a method by which the causes of deterioration can be eliminated. This is done by achieving a state of harmony between the materials and their environment. It is therefore necessary to ascertain, in some detail, the influence of the environment upon the materials in question.

As general interest in toy soldiers increases and they begin to take their place in museums, there is a growing need to ensure that they are exhibited under the right conditions. This chapter will deal with the materials from which toy soldiers are made and the basic problems of deterioration. It must however be made clear that conservation is not a technique of improving the appearance of the object. An improved appearance may of course result from carrying out the conservation procedure correctly, but restoration takes the process a step further; it improves the appearance of the object by replacing lost pieces with substitute materials, and touching-up damaged paintwork. Especially in the case of antique toy soldiers, care should be taken to ensure that restoration, although not glaringly apparent, is detectable. In this way one makes certain that the fine line between restoration and attempted forgery is not crossed.

All too often toy soldiers have been neglected, damaged and allowed to decay. The collector himself can do a great deal to rectify this situation. In addition to the obvious modellers tools such as files, tweezers and adhesives, there are some basic pieces of equipment which will be needed to carry out the work.

1   A small hair or paper hygrometer. This instrument is simply a dial with a single arm like a stop watch. The arm points to the correct Relative Humidity (R.H.) by the hair (or the paper) expanding or contracting thereby indicating the amount of water in the atmosphere. It is an essential piece of equipment. A slightly more expensive version known as a thermohygrometer includes an additional arm to show temperature. The relationship between the two is critical and the R.H. can be changed by altering the temperature, but that is beyond the scope of this chapter.

The importance of these considerations for the serious collector must be stressed. The R.H. fluctuates continually, this causes physical change in the basically unstable materials from which toy soldiers are made, and damage can result.

2   A pin vice. It consists of an adjustable chuck mounted on a wooden handle and is useful when removing hard corrosion on the surface of metal objects. The bit can be ground to give a fine pointed tip or a cutting edge. Corrosion should be sliced away in layers, never dug from the surface of metal objects. Any form of pressure can cause a lot of damage.

3   Hogs hair and sable brushes of varying widths and stiffnesses. They are used to brush off white powder deposits, to apply adhesives and paint, and to clean both composition and paper soldiers.

4   A good craft knife with interchangable scalpel blades for the mechanical cleaning of soldiers, whatever material they are made from. Different sized and shaped blades are essential to suit all the jobs to be done.

5   An illuminated magnifier. This is perhaps the most important item because it is useful at all stages of conservation and for touching up paintwork during restoration.

There are some principles common to the proper conservation of all categories of toy soldiers. These will be looked at before dealing with problems specific to each individual material.

It is important to provide the correct environmental situation, controlled R.H. and temperature, so that a lot of potential problems will never in fact arise. In general the most favourable conditions for metal toy soldiers is the dryest environment possible. Wooden and paper soldiers are best in an R.H. of about 65 per cent. Under no circumstances should the environmental conditions be changed drastically, not even to bring a soldier into the correct conditions. This is because objects which are kept for a long time under the wrong R.H. reach what is called a state of equilibrium. This state stops the deterioration from worsening. Dramatic changes in environmen will cause damage to your collection: any change must be gradual.

Exposure to acid fumes released from oak wood in furniture, show cases, flooring or vinegar must be prevented. Do not therefore keep your collection in a room which has any oak in it or even a vinegar bottle. The air in any normal room contains sulphur dioxide, this when mixed with moisture in the atmosphere will form sulphuric acid having an equally disasterous result on your collection.

Keep your toy soldiers in a ventilated case (not made of oak). It should have dust filters and a small quantity of Silica-gel chrystals which will change colour from purple to opaque white as they absorb moisture from the atmosphere.

Continuous handling can cause damage mainly to paper and metal soldiers largely because of the salts in your hands when the R.H. is high.

Paper Soldiers

Paper is constructed from a group of fibres bonded together by sizing agents of different kinds. The fibres are cellulose and liable to deterioration in many ways.

1 The principal cause is humidity. Paper is a hygroscopic material, this means it will absorb moisture from the atmosphere which in turn will cause damage. This manifests itself in the form of a mould growth on the surface.

2 Over exposure to ultra-violet light from direct sunlight can cause damage. Even on a dull day the amount of ultra-violet can be harmful.

3 Thermal deterioration can be caused by excessively high temperatures from a spot light.

4 High R.H. in combination with poor ventilation will cause what is known as foxing. This is easily identified as brown spots, brought about by micro-organisms living in the size (glue) of the paper. Some of these organisms also live in the cellulose fibres causing the surface of the paper to be eroded, and if not treated will become very brittle. When this kind of deterioration takes

127

place, iron salts, a common impurity in paper, will accumulate on the damaged areas causing foxing.

5   Physical damage caused by tearing, this leaves a feathery edge of exposed fibres.

There are various steps which will be necessary to treat the damage.

1   The symptoms of mould growth are patches of a fine white fluff grey/green in the centre and getting lighter towards the edge. The source of the problem should be tackled first, and that is high humidity. Change the Silica-gel crystals regularly and increase ventilation. Do not raise the temperature in the room, but dry it out thoroughly. The mould should be brushed off the infected areas, but not in the room in which the outbreak happened. It must be done away from the rest of the collection in a laboratory or well ventilated place. A 1 per cent thymol in industrial methylated spirit (IMS) or alcohol solution should be brushed onto the spots.

2   Insects in paper must be treated with a solid insecticide like Gammexane. Some insecticides are very harmful to man and should be used with great care, following the manufacturer's instructions precisely.

3   Foxing is treated with a very mild bleach such as choloramin T, it leaves no harmful remains on the paper and thereby minimises washing. Never use any household bleaches or any bleach of unknown formula. Mix 1 per cent of the choloramin T in distilled water and immerse the paper in it until the brown spots have gone.

4   Oil and fat stains can be removed from the sheet of paper by placing it between two sheets of blotting paper and ironing with a hot iron.

5   If the sheet is torn, back it with Japanese tissue using a cellulose adhesive diluted in acetone (nail varnish remover).

Some paper toy soldiers were hand painted in water colour or gouache. In these cases it is best to get the advice of a professional conservator on the advisability of cleaning. These are a few of the major, but preventable, hazards for paper toy soldiers. To achieve a trouble free collection the following recommendations will have to be followed (as well as the general ones previously mentioned).

1   The collection must be kept at an R.H. not exceeding 60 per cent and at 16°C temperature. To make sure of this it is essential to have a hygrometer in the case.

2   Make sure that your collection of paper soldiers are not under direct sunlight or spot lamps. Remember that even a dull day can produce 60 per cent ultra-violet, the daily average in the north of England, and it will cause colours to fade.

Wooden and Composition Soldiers

The deterioration of wooden and composition soldiers starts for the same reasons as paper soldiers. The same conditions for preservation must be observed. They also have some special problems of their own.

1   A very dry atmosphere can cause shrinkage in composition soldiers, but the wire armature is liable to corrode if the R.H. is too high. This in turn causes the composition to split owing to the expansion of the corroded wire. The ideal R.H. for these pieces is about 50 per cent to minimise the risk of problems arising. This is important, for once the wire has corroded and the soldier split it requires careful restoration.

2   Another problem which might arise is woodworm. This is a tiny wood boring beetle which tunnels into the wood converting it to powder. The result of its activities should be easily observed because of the fresh powder that is dug out in the tunneling process.
    The infected pieces should be isolated in a clear plastic bag and observed in order to ascertain whether the infection is still active. If it is, treatment should start immediately. Commercially available wood worm fluid is brushed into the infected wood. A careful check must be made on any other figures, the case and the room to see if it has spread.

Composition soldiers are particularly prone to crack and often the wire armature may be seen. If this has happened and the crack is small, fill it with Polyfilla (the variety which is ready mixed in a tube). Larger cracks may require the wire armature to be mechanically cleaned and then painted with a cellulose lacquer before being filled by plastic wood or a sawdust/cellulose adhesive mixture.
    Beetle holes after treatment should be impregnated by hypodermic syringe with a commercial wood hardener. The holes can then be filled with beeswax mixed with a pigment to match the surrounding colour.

129

Metal Toy Soldiers

The majority of old metal toy soldiers were made from an alloy of tin and lead, the percentages of each varying from maker to maker.

Because of the different manufacturing processes some of these metals are hydrogenous. Metal structures will also be different depending on the rate of cooling. These and other factors determine whether an individual toy soldier will develop anodic (positive) and cathodic (negative) areas. Stresses may have been set up in the metal during the moulding process, which in the presence of high R.H. will react rather as a battery does with electro-chemical deterioration. This simply means that one part might corrode but not another. It can also happen if soldiers are made from different metals. For instance bases, heads and accoutrements are frequently cast from different metals from the body. A figure coming into contact with a metal pin in a showcase can corrode.

The dull grey appearance of lead objects is due to the presence of metal oxide on the surface. Although this looks unattractive it does serve as a protective film on the metal, preventing deterioration. When deterioration starts a white/grey powder, popularly and wrongly known as lead disease, will show. It is in fact basic lead carbonate. If this is accompanied by a very noticable increase in the size of the object, professional help is urgently needed. However in its early stages the problem can be treated by the collector.

There are three recognised methods:

1   The use of electrochemical reduction. This involves a lot of specialist equipment and expertise and is best left to the expert.

2   The acid treatment. This is dangerous and might cause damage to the paintwork and the casting.

3   The treatment with ion-exchange resin. This resin is commercially available and the treatment is simple. Excess lead carbonate powder should be brushed off the surface and the unaffected areas sealed with soluble nylon or a 10 per cent PVA/IMS solution. The soldier is then laid between layers of the resin and covered with distilled water. Boiled until the carbonate is converted back to metal and coated with a protective layer of clear cellulose lacquer.

To retouch paintwork, enamels such as Humbrol should be used, but do not overpaint old paint. If a casting is broken any of the quick setting epoxy adhesives will adequately join the pieces.

Plastic Soldiers

The deterioration of plastic soldiers is mainly due to their being subjected to excessive heat, causing them to melt, and there is nothing which can be done to help them. All one can do is avoid the causes of deterioration. Do not put them next to heat sources and prevent exposure to solvent vapour.

Plastic soldiers can be broken by rough handling. There are various commercial plastic adhesives available to stick them together.

General Note

If toy soldiers are coated with a 20 per cent PVA/IMS, or cellulose lacquer before painting, or in the case of old ones used as an external finish, it will keep them reasonably free from deterioration problems. It is, of course, important to observe the other precautions laid out in this chapter.

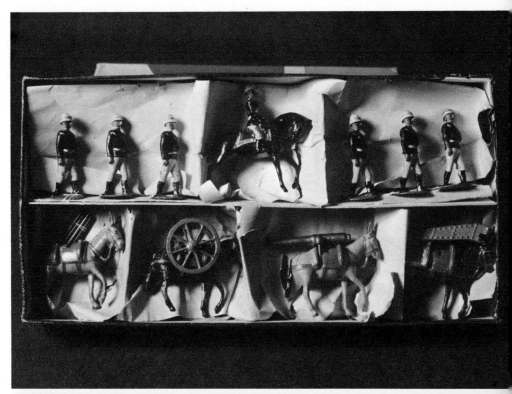

Appendix I: Where to see Toy Soldiers

The museums listed are those with collections of toy (as opposed to model) soldiers. In some cases, especially in Europe, the two kinds are inextricably mixed.

AUSTRIA
Vienna, Kunsthistorisches Museum
  Flats, dioramas.
Vienna, Östereichishes Zinnfigurenmuseum
  Flats, dioramas.

FRANCE
Epinal Museum
  Paper sheets.
Strasbourg Museum
  Mcdieval, paper, flats.
Paris:
Musée de l'Armée
  Paper, flats, semi-solids, solids, hollow-casts, dioramas.
Musée Carnavalet
  Paper soldiers.
Musée de Cluny
  Medieval, 16th & 17th century solids.
Compiëgne
  Wood, flats, solids, dioramas.

GERMANY
Bayer Armeemuseum
  Flats, solids, dioramas.
Celle, Bomann Museum
  Early flats, solids.
Dresden, Armeemuseum der Deutschen Demokratischen Republik
  Flats, dioramas.
Hanover, Historic Museum
  Flats, dioramas.

Kulmbach, Deutsches Zinnfigurenmuseum
  Wood, paper, early flats, flats, solids, dioramas.
  Altogether some 250,000 figures.
Leipzig, Museum für Geschichte der Stadt
  Flats, dioramas.
Nurnberg, Germanisches Nationalmuseum
  Early flats, flats, dioramas.
Schwerin, Historisches Museum
  Paper, early flats, flats, dioramas.
Thüringen, Deutsches Spielzeugmuseum
  Flats, dioramas.
Weimar, Statdmuseum
  Flats, dioramas.

GREAT BRITAIN
Dorking Museum, Surrey
  Automata.
Edinburgh, Museum of Childhood
  Wood, flats, semi-solids, solids, hollow-cast, composition.
Lewes, Sussex, Anne of Cleve's House
  Solids, hollow-casts.
Luton Museum, Bedfordshire
  Wood, flats, semi-solids.
Norwich, Strangers' Hall Museum
  Wood, wooden trellis toys, solids, hollow-casts.
Rottingdean, Sussex, Rottingdean Grange & National Toy Museum
  Wood, solids, hollow-casts.
Sudbury, Derbyshire, Sudbury Hall
  Wood, paper, flats.
Tunbridge Wells Museum, Kent
  Flats, semi-solid, solid, hollow-casts.
Woodstock, Oxfordshire, Blenheim Palace
  Solids.
London:
Bethnal Green Museum
  Flats, solids, hollow-casts, composition.
The London Museum, Kensington Palace
  Wood, paper, flats, solids, hollow-casts.
Pollock's Toy Museum
  Paper, hollow-casts.

HOLLAND
Leyden, Royal Dutch Army Museum
Paper, flats, solids.
Altogether some 30,000 flats and solids, and 10,500 paper.

ITALY
Milan Museum
Flats.
Naples Museum
Paper.

SWITZERLAND
Coppet Castle
Flats.
Grandson Castle
Paper, solids, dioramas.
Zurich Landesmuseum
Flats.

UNITED STATES OF AMERICA
Detroit Children's Museum
Wood, solids, hollow-casts.
New York Museum
Wood, paper, solids, hollow-casts.

USSR
Hermitage Museum, Leningrad
Wood, paper, flats.

Appendix II: List of Britains' Figures

Between 1893 and 1918 Britains produced their first two hundred boxes of best quality toy soldiers. Sets on the following list were available about 1940 except for those marked with an asterisk which had been withdrawn, and are only shown to complete the early total. There is also a list of sets from the 'B' series. The number at the end of the description of each box denotes the quantity of soldiers it contained.

Box
1   Life Guards, 5
2   Royal Horse Guards, 5
3   5th Dragoon Guards (Princess Charlotte of Wales'), 5
4   Selection from Boxes 1, 2 and 3 painted gold*
5   Ditto*
6   Boer Cavalry*
7   7th Royal Fusiliers; at the slope; with officer, 8 (large size figure)
8   4th Hussars (Queen's Own), 5
9   Fusiliers*
10 Salvation Army*
11 Black Watch (Royal Highlanders); charging, 8
12 11th Hussars (Prince Albert's Own), 5
13 3rd Hussars (King's Own), 5
14 Salvation Army*
15 Argyll & Sutherland Highlanders; charging, 8
16 East Kent Regiment (the Buffs); on guard; with officer, bugler and drummer, 8
17 Somerset Light Infantry; on guard; with officer and bugler, 8
18 Worcestershire Regiment; on guard; with officer and drummer, 8
19 West India Regiment; marching; with officer, 7
20 Russian and Japanese cavalry and infantry*
21 Selection of Life Guards, 11th Hussars, Scots Guards and East Kent Regiment, 27
22 Selection of Royal Horse Guards, 16/5th Lancers, Black Watch and Worcestershire Regiment, 27
23 5th Royal Irish Lancers*
24 9th Lancers (Queen's Royal), 5

25   Soldiers to Shoot*
26   Boer Infantry*
27   Band of the Line, 12
28   Mountain Artillery with mules, officer, gunners, gun and ammunition, 12
29   Selection of Mountain Artillery, Life Guards, 3rd Hussars, 9th Lancers and Royal West Surrey Regiment, 41
30   Drums and Bugles of the Line, 7
31   1st Dragoons (Royal), 5
32   2nd Dragoons (Royal Scots Greys), 5
33   16/5th Lancers, 5
34   Grenadier Guards; standing firing; with officer and drummer, 7
35   Royal Marines; at the slope; with officer, 8
36   Royal Sussex Regiment; at the slope; with mounted officer, 7
37   Full Band of the Coldstream Guards, 21
38   Dr Jameson and the South African Mounted Infantry, 5
39   Royal Horse Artillery with gun, limber, team and escort galloping, 13
40   Selection of 1st Dragoons and Somerset Light Infantry, 14
41   Selection of 2nd Dragoons and Grenadier Guards, 14
42   Selection of Life Guards and Royal Sussex Regiment, with mounted officer, 12
43   2nd Life Guards; at the gallop; 5
44   2nd Dragoon Guards (Queen's Bays), 5
45   3rd Madras Cavalry (Indian Army); review order; with trumpeter, 5
46   Hodson's Horse (4th Duke of Cambridge's Own Lancers, Indian Army); with trumpeter, 5
47   Skinner's Horse (1st Duke of York's Own Cavalry, Indian Army); with trumpeter, 5
48   Egyptian Camel Corps, 6
49   South Australian Lancers, with officer, 5
50   Selection of Life Guards and 4th Hussars, 10
51   Selection of 11th Hussars and 16/5th Lancers, 10
52   Selection of 16/5th Lancers and Life Guards, 10
53   Selection of Royal Horse Guards, 4th Hussars and Grenadier Guards, 18
54   Selection of Life Guards, 2nd Dragoon Guards and 9th Lancers, 15
55   Selection of 2nd Dragoons, 3rd Hussars and 16/5th Lancers, 15
56   Selection of Grenadier Guards and East Kent Regiment, 15
57   1st Dragoon Guards (small size)*
58   Selection of Royal Horse Guards, 2nd Dragoons and Mounted Infantry*
59   2nd Dragoons (Royal Scots Greys), 10
60   1st Bombay Lancers (Indian Army)*
61   3rd Madras Cavalry (Indian Army)*
62   Skinner's Horse (Indian Army); with trumpeter, 10
63   Hodson's Horse (Indian Army); with officer and trumpeter, 10
64   Selection of 27th Light Cavalry and 2nd Madras Regiment (Indian Army); at the slope, 8

65   Russian Cavalry and Infantry*
66   13th Duke of Connaught's Own Lancers (Indian Army); with trumpeter, 5
67   Corps of Madras Pioneers (Indian Army); at the slope, 8
68   2nd Bombay Grenadiers (Indian Army); at the slope, 8
69   Pipers of the Scots Guards, 6
70   Scots Guards*
71   Turkish Cavalry; review order; with officer, 5
72   Life Guards; uniforms of present day and 1815*
73   Selection of Royal Artillery, Life Guards, 17th Lancers, Royal Welsh Fusiliers, 2nd Dragoons, Band of the Line, Gordon Highlanders and General Officer, 73
74   Royal Welsh Fusiliers; at the slope; with officer and goat mascot, 8
75   Scots Guards; at the slope; with officer and piper, 8
76   Middlesex Regiment; at the slope; with officer, 8
77   Gordon Highlanders; at the slope; with piper, 8
78   Bluejackets; running at the trail; with officer and petty officer, 8
79   Naval Landing Party with gun and limber, 11
80   Whitejackets; running at the trail; with officer, 8
81   17th Lancers (Duke of Cambridge's Own), 5
82   Scots Guards with colours and pioneers, 7
83   Middlesex Yeomanry, 5
84   Selection of Life Guards, and 7th Royal Fusiliers (small size)*
85   Selection of 5th Dragoon Guards, 2nd Dragoons, Scots Guards and Northumberland Fusiliers (small size)*
86   Lancashire Fusiliers (small size)*
87   13th Hussars (small size)*
88   Seaforth Highlanders with pipers, 16
89   Cameron Highlanders; standing, kneeling and lying firing; 24
90   Coldstream Guards; standing, kneeling and lying firing; 27
91   USA Infantry; on guard, federal dress; with officer, 8
92   Spanish Infantry; at the slope; with officer, 8
93   Selection of Royal Horse Guards and Coldstream Guards with band, colours, pioneers and officers, 71
94   21st Lancers (Empress of India's), 5
95   Selection of Japanese Cavalry and Infantry; review order; 13
96   York & Lancaster Regiment; running at the trail; with officer, 8
97   Royal Marines; running at the trail; with officer, 8
98   Kings Royal Rifle Corps; running at the trail; with officer, 8
99   13th Hussars, 5
100 21st Lancers (Empress of India's); review order; 5
101 Life Guards Band, 12
102 Selection of Grenadier, Coldstream, Scots and Irish Guards with mounted officer, 32
103 Band of the Royal Horse Guards*
104 City Imperial Volunteers; on guard; with officer, 9
105 Imperial Yeomanry, 5
106 Selection of 6th Dragoon Guards and 6th Carabiniers, 5

107 Irish Guards; at the slope; with officer, 8
108 6th Dragoons (Inniskillings), 5
109 Royal Dublin Fusiliers; marching at the trail; 8
110 Devonshire Regiment; marching at the trail; 8
111 Grenadier Guards; attention; with mounted officer, 7
112 Seaforth Highlanders; at the slope; 8
113 East Yorkshire Regiment; attention; 8
114 Cameron Highlanders; at the slope; 8
115 Egyptian Cavalry, 5
116 Sudanese Infantry; at the trail; 8
117 Egyptian Infantry; attention; 8
118 Gordon Highlanders; lying firing; with officer, 8
119 Gloucestershire Regiment*
120 Coldstream Guards; kneeling firing; with officer, 8
121 Royal West Surrey Regiment; standing firing; with officer, 8
122 Black Watch (Royal Highlanders); standing firing; with officer, 8
123 Bikanir Camel Corps (Indian Army); 6
124 Irish Guards; lying firing; with officer, 8
125 Royal Horse Artillery (small size)*
126 Royal Horse Artillery (small size)*
127 4/7th Dragoon Guards, 5
128 12th Royal Lancers (Prince of Wales'); 5
129 Selection of 12th Lancers, 2nd Dragoons, 1st Dragoon Guards, 11th Hussars and 2nd Life Guards, 70*
130 Scots Guards; marching, running, attention and standing, kneeling and lying firing; with pipers, drum and bugle band, colours and pioneers, mounted and dismounted officers, 118
131 Selection of Royal Horse Artillery, Mountain Artillery, British Camel Corps, 2nd Dragoons, 11th Hussars, 5th Dragoon Guards, 17th Lancers, 2nd Life Guards, Royal Horse Guards, Band of the Coldstream Guards, Scots Guards; standing, kneeling and lying firing; Gordon Highlanders with pipers, Worcestershire Regiment, Bluejackets and Whitejackets with naval gun, and General Officer, 274*
132 Selection of Royal Horse Artillery, Mountain Artillery, 2nd Dragoons, 11th Hussars, 12th Lancers, 2nd Life Guards, Royal Horse Guards, 7th Dragoon Guards, Band of the Line, Seaforth Highlanders with pipers, Royal Welsh Fusiliers with goat, Coldstream Guards; standing, kneeling and lying firing; East Kent Regiment, Naval gun and General Officer, 167*
133 Russian Infantry*
134 Japanese Infantry; charging, review order; 8
135 Japanese Cavalry; review order; with officer, 5
136 Cossacks (Russian Army)*
137 Royal Army Medical Corps with doctors and nurses, 24
138 French Cuirassiers; review order; with officer, 5
139 French Chasseurs à Cheval; review order; with officer, 5
140 French Dragoons; review order; with officer, 5

141 French Infanterie de Ligne; at the slope; 8
142 French Zouaves; charging, review order; 8
143 French Matelots*
144 Royal Field Artillery; at the walk; with gun, limber and team, 9
145 Royal Army Medical Corps with ambulance waggon, 7
146 Royal Army Service Corps with waggon, 5
147 Zulus of Africa, 8
148 Royal Lancaster Regiment*
149 American Soldiers*
150 North American Indians; on foot; with chief, 8
151 Royal Naval Reserve; shoulder arms; with petty officer, 8
152 North American Indians; mounted; 5
153 Prussian Hussars; review order; with officer, 5
154 Prussian Infantry; at the slope, review order; 8
155 Railway Staff*
156 Royal Irish Regiment; standing, kneeling and lying firing; 8
157 Gordon Highlanders; standing, kneeling and lying firing; 8
158 Railway Staff*
159 Territorial Army Yeomanry, 5
160 Territorials; at the trail; with officer, 8
161 Boy Scouts with Scout Master, 8
162 Boy Scout Camp, 23
163 Boy Scout Signallers, 5
164 Arabs on Horses, 5
165 Italian Cavalry; review order; with officer, 5
166 Italian Infantry; at the slope, review order; with officer, 8
167 Turkish Infantry; on guard, review order; 8
168 Civilians*
169 Italian Bersaglieri; marching, slung rifles, review order; 8
170 Greek Cavalry; review order; with officer, 5
171 Greek Infantry; marching at the trail, review order; with officer, 8
172 Bulgarian Infantry; marching at the trail, review order; with officer, 8
173 Serbian Infantry; review order*
174 Montenegrin Infantry; review order*
175 Austrian Lancers with officer and trumpeter, 5
176 Austrian Dragoons with officer and trumpeter, 5
177 Austrian Line Infantry; at the slope; 8
178 Austrian Foot Guards; at the slope; 8
179 Cowboys; mounted; 5
180 Boy Scout Display, 22
181 Boy Scout Display*
182 11th Hussars (Prince Albert's Own); dismounted with horses; 8
183 Cowboys on foot; 8
184 Cowboys; mounted and on foot; 15
185 Wild West Display, 30
186 Mexican Infantry; marching, slung rifles, review order; with officer, 8

187 Arabs on foot, 8
188 Zulu Kraal with warriors, palms and scenic background, 11
189 Belgian Infantry; on guard, review order; 8
190 Belgian Cavalry; review order; with officer, 5
191 French Turcos; charging, review order; 8
192 French Infanterie; at the slope, steel helmets; with officer, 8
193 Arabs on Camels, 6
194 Machine Gun Section; lying; 8
195 Infantry of the Line; at the trail, steel helmets; with officer, 8
196 Greek Evzones; at the slope, review order; 8
197 Ghurka Rifles (1st King George's Own, the Malaun Regiment); marching at the trail, 8
198 Machine Gun Section; sitting; 6
199 Motor Cycle Machine Gunner; with sidecar*
200 Motor Cycle Dispatch Rider*
201 Mounted Officers of the General Staff, 4
202 Togoland Warriors with bows and arrows, 8
205 Coldstream Guards; present arms; with officer, 8
206 Warwickshire Regiment; present arms; with officer, 8
208 North American Indians; mounted and on foot; with chief, 13
209 Cowboys; mounted and on foot; 13
210 North American Indians; mounted and on foot; with trees, 15
211 Horse drawn heavy howitzer mounted on tractor wheels
212 Royal Scots; at the slope; 8
213 Highland Light Infantry; at the slope; 8
214 Royal Canadian Mounted Police; dismounted, at the slope, winter dress; 8
215 Selection of French Infanterie; standing, kneeling and lying firing, steel helmets; with machine gunners and officer, 14
216 Argentinian Infantry; at the slope, review order; 8
217 Argentinian Cavalry; review order; with officer, 5
218 Spanish Cavalry; review order; with officer, 5
219 Argentinian Military School Cadets; at the slope; 8
220 Uruguayan Cavalry; review order; with officer, 5
221 Uruguayan Military School Cadets; at the slope; 8
222 Uruguayan Infantry; at the slope, review order; 8
223 Arabs; mounted and on foot; 13
224 Arabs; on foot, horses and camels; with palms, 11
225 King's African Rifles; at the slope; 8
226 USA West Point Cadets; at the slope, winter dress; 8
227 USA Infantry; at the slope, service dress; with officer, 8
228 USA Marines; at the slope, blue uniform; with officer, 8
229 USA Cavalry; service dress; 5
230 USA Sailors; at the slope, bluejackets; 8
232 Selection of USA Infantry, Marines and West Point Cadets, 24
233 Selection of USA Infantry, Cavalry, Marines and West Point Cadets, 29

240   Royal Air Force personnel, 8
241   Chinese Infantry; charging with sword, review order; 8
242   USA Infantry; at the slope; with mounted officer, 7
244   North American Indians; mounted and on foot; with chief, 7
245   Cowboys; mounted and on foot; 7
246   Selection of 2nd Dragoons and Scots Guards, 7
247   Arabs; mounted and on foot; 7
248   Selection of Life Guards and Middlesex Regiment, 7
249   Selection of British Infantry and Cavalry, 7
250   Selection of 2nd Dragoon Guards and Grenadier Guards, 7
251   Selection of 21st Lancers and Royal Fusiliers, 7
253   Welsh Guards with mounted officer, 8
254   Selection of Bluejackets and Whitejackets; shoulder arms; with petty officer, 9
255   Green Howards (Princess Alexandra of Wales's Own Yorkshire Regiment); 9
256   Cowboys; mounted and on foot; 17
257   North American Indians; mounted and on foot; 17
258   Infantry of the Line; at the trail, steel helmets; with officer, 8
261   USA Marines; blue uniform; 16
265   Selection of USA Marines, Bluejackets and Whitejackets; 24
267   Selection of USA Infantry and Cavalry; service dress; 13
270   11th Hussars; mounted and dismounted; 12
272   Selection of North American Indians and Cowboys; mounted and on foot; 13
273   Selection of North American Indians and Cowboys; mounted and on foot; 15
274   North American Indians; mounted and on foot; 7
275   Cowboys; mounted and on foot; 7
276   USA Cavalry; at the gallop, service dress; 5
281   North American Indians; mounted and on foot; with bell tent, 8
282   Cowboys; mounted and on foot; with bell tent, 8
283   Selection of USA Infantry and Cavalry; service dress; with bell tent, 8
284   Selection of USA Infantry and Cavalry; service dress; 21
287   Selection of USA Infantry and Cavalry; service dress; 7
288   Selection of USA Marines and Sailors; 16
290   Selection of USA Infantry and Cavalry; service dress; 13
291   Selection of USA Infantry and Cavalry; service dress; 26
294   Selection of USA Infantry; service dress; and Marines, 16
299   USA West Point Cadets; at the slope, summer dress; 8
300   Arabs; mounted and on foot; 17
301   Arabs; mounted and on foot; with bell tent, 8
302   Selection of 2nd Dragoons and Scots Guards with bell tent; 8
303   Selection of Life Guards and Middlesex Regiment with bell tent, 8
304   Territorials; mounted and on foot; with bell tent, 8
305   North American Indians; mounted and on foot, 10
306   Cowboys; mounted and on foot; 10

307 Arabs; mounted and on foot; 10
309 Selection of 2nd Dragoons and Scots Guards, 10
310 Selection of Life Guards and Middlesex Regiment, 10
311 Territorials; mounted and on foot; 10
312 Grenadier Guards; at the slope, winter overcoats; with officer, 8
313 Gunners, Royal Regiment of Artillery; steel helmets; 8
314 Coldstream Guards; at ease; with officers, 8
315 10th Hussars, 5
316 Royal Horse Artillery; standing; with gun, limber and team, 9
317 Royal Field Artillery; standing; with gun, limber and team, 9
318 Horsed Gun Team, Royal Artillery; standing and kneeling gunners, steel helmets; 17
320 Royal Army Medical Corps, doctors and nurses, 8
321 Drum and Fife Band of the Line, 17
322 Coldstream Guards with Drum and Fife Band, 25
323 Selection of USA Cavalry, Artillery, Marines, Sailors, Infantry of the Line, West Point Cadets; winter and summer dress; dispatch rider and officers, 73
324 Selection of USA Marines, Sailors, Infantry of the Line, West Point Cadets, machine gunners, cavalry, infantry in gas masks, and officers, 81
329 Guardsman with sentry box; 2
338 Infantry; service dress, steel helmets, gas masks; 16
341 Machine Gun Section; lying; 16
347 USA Infantry; at the slope, service dress; with officer and tent, 10
348 USA West Point Cadets; at the slope, review order; with tent, 10
349 USA Marines; at the slope; with tent, 10
350 North American Indians; on foot; with chief and tent, 10
359 USA Machine Gun Section; lying; 8
399 USA Marines; at the slope, active service dress; 9
400 Life Guards; winter dress; 5
407 Selection of Whitejackets and Bluejackets; running at the trail; with officers, 16
424 USA West Point Cadets; winter and summer dress; 16
427 Selection of French Cuirassiers and Infanterie de Ligne; review order; 13
429 Selection of Scots Guards and Life Guards; winter dress; 13
430 Life Guards; summer and winter dress; 10
431 Scots Guards; summer and winter dress; 16
432 German Infantry; at the slope, active service dress, steel helmets; 8
433 Monoplane with pilot and hanger
434 Monoplane with pilot and hanger and six aircraftsmen
435 USA Monoplane with pilot and hanger
436 USA Monoplane with pilot and hanger and six aircraftsmen
437 Officers of the Gordon Highlanders; foot and mounted; 5
460 Scots Guards colour party and standard, 7
1201 Gun of the Royal Artillery

1203	Tank of the Royal Tank Corps; Carden Loyd type; with driver and machine gunner, 4
1250	Royal Tank Corps; marching; with officer, 8
1251	USA Infantry; standing, kneeling and lying firing, active service dress; with officer, 9
1252	Cowboys; standing and kneeling firing; 8
1253	USA Whitejackets; at the slope; 8
1257	Yeomen of the Guard with Governor, 9
1258	Knights in Armour with squires and herald, 6
1260	Infantry; standing, kneeling and lying firing, peaked caps, 9
1263	Gun of the Royal Artillery
1264	Naval Gun, 4.7″, mounted for field operations
1265	Heavy Howitzer, 18″, mounted for garrison work
1266	Heavy Howitzer, 18″, mounted on tractor wheels
1267	Selection of Royal Scots, Scots Guards with pipers, Gordon Highlanders, 2nd Dragoons, Middlesex Regiment, 12th Lancers, Life Guards, 5th Dragoon Guards, 11th Hussars, and with mounted and foot officers, 83
1283	Grenadier Guards; standing, kneeling and lying firing; 8
1284	Royal Marines; at the slope, running at the trail; with officers, 16
1285	Territorials, yeomanry and infantry, 13
1286	Infantry; standing, kneeling and lying firing, peak caps; 25
1287	British Military Band; peak caps; with Drum Major, 21
1288	Royal Marine band with drum major, 21
1289	Royal Artillery Gunners; steel helmets; with gun and officers
1290	Band of the Line; Peak Caps; with Drum Major, 12
1291	Royal Marine Band with Drum Major, 12
1292	Gun of the Royal Artillery
1293	Durban Light Infantry; at the slope; with officer, 8
1294	Infantry; at the slope, tropical service dress; 8
1300	Selection of Royal Army Medical Corps; hospital marquee with doctors, nurses, stretcher-bearers and wounded; Royal Army Service Corps with waggon; Royal Army Medical Corps with ambulance waggon, 42
1301	USA Military Band with Drum Major, 12
1302	USA Military Band; service dress; with Drum Major, 21
1307	Knights; mounted and on foot; 7
1308	Knights; mounted and on foot; 11
1311	Selection of North American Cowboys and Indians; foot; 8
1312	Selection of North American Cowboys and Indians; mounted; 5
1313	Eastern people with animals and palms, 12
1314	Eastern people with animals and palms 20
1318	Machine Gun Section; sitting and lying; 7
1319	Machine Gun Section; sitting and lying; with officer, 14
1320	Infantry; lying firing, peak caps; with officer, 9
1321	Armoured Car with swivelling gun and rubber tyres
1322	Carden Loyd Tank, with squad of Royal Tank Corps and officer, 7

1323 Selection of 7th Royal Fusiliers, Seaforth Highlanders, Royal Sussex
      Regiment, and with mounted and foot officers, 23
1324 Selection of Scots Guards with piper, Middlesex Regiment with
      officer, Royal Scots, 24
1325 Gordon Highlanders; standing, kneeling and lying firing; 16
1326 Selection of Irish Guards with Officer and Gordon Highlanders with
      piper, 16
1327 Coldstream Guards; standing, kneeling and lying firing; 17
1328 Infantry; standing, kneeling and lying firing, peak caps; 18
1329 Royal Army Service Corps General Service Waggon, 4
1330 Royal Engineers General Service Waggon, 4
1331 Royal Engineers; steel helmets; General Service Waggon, 4
1334 4 wheeled army lorry; rubber tyres, tipping body; with driver
1335 6 wheeled army lorry; rubber tyres, tipping body; with driver
1339 Royal Artillery; at the gallop, steel helmets; with gun, limber, team
      and escort, 13
1342 7th Rajput Regiment (Duke of Connaught's Own, Indian Army); at
      the slope; 8
1343 Royal Horse Guards; winter dress; 5
1349 Royal Canadian Mounted Police; mounted, summer dress; with
      officer, 5
1350 Selection of Gordon Highlanders with pipers, 2nd Dragoons, Scots
      Guards, Royal Scots, Life Guards, 11th Hussars, and with mounted
      and foot officers
1358 Selection of Belgian Cavalry and Infantry; review order; 16
1366 French Infanterie; standing, kneeling and lying firing, active service
      dress, steel helmets; with machine gunners; 7
1368 Selection of Italian Bersaglieri and cavalry; review order; 13
1379 Belgian Cavalry; service dress; 5
1382 Selection of Belgian Cavalry and Infantry; service dress; 13
1383 Belgian Infantry; standing, kneeling and lying firing, service dress;
      with machine gunners, 14
1384 Belgian Infantry; standing, kneeling and lying firing; service dress;
      with machine gunners, 21
1387 French Infanterie; standing, kneeling and lying firing; with machine
      gunners and officer, 21
1389 Belgian Infantry; at the slope, service dress; 8
1392 British Army co-operation Autogiro, Cierva C30
1395 Kings Own Scottish Borderers; at the slope; 8
1407 Selection of 21st Lancers, Territorial Yeomanry and Infantry, British
      Infantry with steel helmets, British Infantry with gas masks, machine
      gunners, officers bandsmen and buglers, 72
1424 Bodyguard of the Emperor of Abyssinia; attention; 8
1425 Abyssinian Tribesmen; at the slope; 8
1432 Covered 10 wheel army tender; rubber tyres; with driver
1433 Covered army tender; caterpillar type; with driver
1434 Abyssinian Royal Bodyguard and Tribesmen, 16

1435	Italian Infantry; at the slope, steel helmets; 8
1436	Italian Infantry; at the slope, colonial service dress; 8
1437	Italian Carabinieri; at the slope, review order; 8
1438	Italian Infantry; at the slope, colonial service dress; 16
1440	Royal Artillery; walking, steel helmets; with gun, limber and team, 9
1448	Staff Car with two officers
1450	Royal Army Medical Corps; steel helmets; with ambulance waggon, 7
1460	Royal Army Service Corps with waggon
1462	Covered Lorry; caterpillar type; with gun, limber and two drivers
1470	State Coach of England with team, 11
1474	Coronation chair
1475	Yeomen of the Guard, walking outriders and footmen of the Royal Household, 18
1476	State Coach of England; with Yeomen of the Guard, walking outriders and Footmen of the Royal Household; 29
1477	State Coach of England; with Yeomen of the Guard, walking outriders, Footman of the Royal Household, staff officers, guards and police; 75
1479	Limber, short pole
1510	Sailors; marching, regulation dress; 8
1512	Army Motor Ambulance; rubber tyres; with driver, wounded man and stretcher
1515	Coldstream Guards; at the slope; with officer, 8
1516	Waterloo Period Line Infantry (1815); carrying pikes, attention; with officer, 8
1517	Waterloo Period Highlanders (1815); carrying pikes, attention; with officer, 8
1518	Waterloo Period Line Infantry (1815); carrying muskets, attention; with officer, 8
1519	Waterloo Period Highlanders (1815); carrying muskets, attention; with officer, 8
1521	Biplane with pilot and hanger
1522	Anti-aircraft gun, 4.5"
1525	USA Biplane with pilot and hanger
1537	Territorials; at the slope, blue uniform; with officer, 8
1538	Territorials; at the slope, green uniform; with officer, 8
1540	Territorials; present arms, blue uniform; with officer, 8
1541	Territorials; present arms, green uniform; with officer, 8
1542	New Zealand Infantry; at the slope, service dress; with officer, 8
1543	New Zealand Infantry; present arms, service dress; with officer, 8
1544	Australian Infantry; at the slope, service dress; with officer, 8
1545	Australian Infantry; present arms, service dress; with officer, 8
1554	Royal Canadian Mounted Police; marching, summer dress; with officer, 8
1555	Changing of the Guard; Scots and Coldstream Guards with officers, standards, band and sentry boxes, 83
1603	Eiren Infantry; at the slope, review order; with officer, 8

1607   Selection of 2nd Dragoons, Scots Guards with standard, piper and officer, sentry boxes with sentries and band, 45

1608   Selection of British Infantry and Cavalry with dispatch riders and machine gunners, 43

1610   Royal Marines; present arms; with officer, 8

1611   British Infantry; prone, service dress, fixed bayonets, gas masks; with officer, 8

1612   British Infantry; throwing grenades, service dress, gas masks; with officer, 8

1613   British Infantry; charging, service dress, fixed bayonets, gas masks; with officer, 7

1614   Selection of British Infantry; throwing grenades, charging, prone, digging, service dress, gas masks; with lying machine gunners and officer, 24

1615   Selection of British Infantry; throwing grenades, charging, prone, digging, service dress, gas masks; with officer, 15

1616   Selection of British Infantry; throwing grenades, charging, prone, service dress, gas masks; with machine gunners and officer, 15

1617   Line Regiments, Regular Army & Territorial; blue uniform; with officer, 8

1618   Rifle Regiments, Regular Army & Territorial; green uniform; with officer, 8

1619   Royal Marines; at the slope, tropical dress; with officer, 8

1620   Royal Marine Light Infantry; at the slope; with officer, 8

1621   Selection of 12th Frontier Force Regiment and Sikhs (Indian Army); at the slope; 8

1622   Royal Marine Light Infantry Band with drum major, 21

1623   USA Infantry; prone, service dress, fixed bayonets, gas masks; with officer, 8

1624   USA Infantry; throwing grenades, service dress, gas masks; with officer, 8

1625   USA Infantry; charging, service dress, fixed bayonets, gas masks; with officer, 7

1626   Selection of USA Infantry; throwing grenades, charging, prone, digging, service dress, gas masks; with lying machine gunners and officer, 24

1627   Selection of USA Infantry; throwing grenades, charging, prone, digging, service dress, gas masks; with officer, 15

1628   Selection of USA Infantry; throwing grenades, charging, prone, service dress, gas masks; with machine gunners and officer, 15

1629   Lord Strathcona's Horse (Canada); review order; with officer, 5

1630   Royal Canadian Dragoons; review order; with officer; 5

1631   Governor General's Horse Guards (Canada); review order; with officer, 5

1632   Royal Canadian Regiment; review order; with officer, 8

1633   Princess Patricia's Canadian Light Infantry; at the slope, review order; with officer, 8

1634   Governor General's Foot Guards (Canada); at the slope, review order; with officer, 8

1635   Selection of Lord Strathcona's Horse and the Royal Canadian Regiment; review order; with officers, 8

1636   Selection of Princess Patricia's Canadian Light Infantry and the Royal Canadian Dragoons; review order; with officers, 13

1637   Selection of Governor General's Horse and Foot Guards (Canada); review order; with officers, 13

1638   Sound Locator & Operator

1639   Range Finder & Operator

1640   Searchlight

1641   Heavy Duty Lorry; 18 wheels, rubber tyres; with driver

1642   Heavy Duty Lorry; 18 wheels, rubber tyres; with driver and searchlight

1643   Heavy Duty Lorry; 18 wheels, rubber tyres; with driver and anti-aircraft gun

1648   Naval Landing Party, Bluejackets and Whitejackets; running at the trail; Bluejackets in regulation dress; with officer and petty officers, 51

1711   French Foreign Legion with mounted officer, 7

1712   French Foreign Legion with mounted officer, 15

1715   Light anti-aircraft gun, 2pdr.

1716   Chassis with wheels for No 1715

1717   Light Anti-aircraft Gun mounted on chassis

1718   Searchlight

1719   Royal Army Medical Corps stretcher party; service dress; 4

1720   2nd Dragoons Mounted Band, 7

1721   2nd Dragoons Mounted Full Band with officer, 12

1722   Scots Guards Pipe Band, 21

1723   Royal Army Medical Corps Stretcher Party; service dress; with nurses, 9

1724   Anti-aircraft Unit; searchlight, sound locator, spotting chairs, tent and 10-wheeled tender, 15

1725   Howitzer, 4.5"

1726   Limber with rubber tyres

1727   Mobile Howitzer Unit with limber and caterpillar tender

1728   Predictor and Operator; service dress

1729   Height Finder and Operator

1730   Royal Artillery Gunners; carrying shells, service dress; 7

1731   Spotting Chair and Observer; service dress

1758   Royal Air Force Fighters, 8

1759   Air Raid Precautions, stretcher party and decontamination men; regulation dress; 9

1791   Royal Corps of Signals, dispatch riders on motor cycles; 4

1793   Machine Gun Corps, motor cyclist & sidecar machine gunner

1794   Infantry; service dress; equipment operators; 8

1824   Selection of British Army nurses, orderlies, stretcher party, predictor and operator, sound locator and operator, range finder and operator, spotting chair and observer, 4.5″ howitzer and limber, caterpillar tender with driver, motor ambulance, 2pdr anti-aircraft gun on chassis and searchlight on chassis, 36

1831   Royal Artillery gun and short pole limber
1832   Motor Tender; 10 wheels, rubber tyres; with 2pdr anti-aircraft gun on chassis
1833   Motor Tender; 10 wheels, rubber tyres; with searchlight on chassis
1854   British Infantry; at the slope, forage cap; 8
1855   Barrage balloon & winch lorry
1856   Polish Infantry; at the slope; 8
1858   British Infantry; slung rifles, battle dress; 8
1859   Sentry Box with sentry
1876   Bren Gun Carrier with driver, gunner and guard
1877   Beetle Lorry and driver
1879   Lorry and Trailer with hydrogen cylinders for use with No 1855
1892   Indian Army Infantry; at the trail, service dress; with officer, 8
1893   Royal Indian Army Service Corps; service dress; with officer and mule, 7
1894   Royal Air Force Pilots and Women's Auxilliary Air Force, 8
1895   German Luftwaffe pilots; full flying kit; 8
1896   Royal Army Medical Corps stretcher party; service dress; 8
1897   Motor Ambulance with doctor, nurses, orderlies and wounded, 18
1898   British Infantry; carrying rifles and tommy guns, service dress; with officer, 8
1900   Union of South Africa, Regiment Louw Wepener; at the slope, service dress; with officer, 8
1901   Union of South Africa, Cape Town Highlanders; at the slope, service dress; with officer, 8
1902   Union of South Africa, Infantry Defence Forces; at the slope, service dress; with officer, 8
1903   Indian Army Mountain Battery; service dress; with gun, gunners, mules and mounted officer, 12
1904   USA Army Air Corps officers and men, 8
1905   USA Army Air Corps pilots, officers and men, 16
1907   British Army Staff Officers; active service order; with dispatch rider, 5
1908   Selection of Officers of the General Staff, guards, line infantry, light infantry, fusiliers and rifles, 8
1909   Royal Army Medical Corps; doctors, nurses, orderlies, wounded, stretchers, tent, ambulance, car and lorry, 28
1910   Royal Army Medical Corps; battle dress; field hospital staff with wounded, 24
1911   Royal Navy; blue and white uniforms; officers and petty officers; 7
1914   Air Raid Precautions Wardens; regulation uniform; 8
1918   Home Guard; marching with slung rifles; 8

List of the 'B' Series

1B	1st Life Guards
2B	Royal Horse Guards
3B	5th Dragoon Guards
4B	Scots Guards
5B	1st Dragoon Guards
6B	2nd Dragoons (Royal Scots Greys)
7B	2nd Life Guards
8B	7th Royal Fusiliers
9B	13th Hussars
10B	11th Hussars
11B	Japanese Cavalry
12B	16th Lancers; active service dress
13B	17th Lancers
14B	Russian Cossacks
15B	Mounted Infantry
16B	Coldstream Guards
17B	Lancashire Fusiliers
18B	Grenadier Guards
19B	Dublin Fusiliers
20B	Manchester Regiment
21B	Northumberland Fusiliers
22B	Royal Navy Bluejackets
23B	Cameron Highlanders; active service dress
24B	Royal Navy Whitejackets
25B	Japanese Infantry
26B	Russian Infantry
125	Royal Artillery gun team; review order
126	Royal Artillery gun team; active service order

Appendix III: Where to buy Toy Soldiers

SHOPS:

Soldiers
36 Kennington Road
London SE1

Tradition
188 Piccadilly
London W1

Under Two Flags
4 St Christopher's Place, Wigmore Street
London W1

BY POST:

Shamus O D Wade
37 Davis Road, Acton
London W3

AUCTION:

Phillips, Son & Neale
Blenstock House, 7 Blenheim Street, New Bond Street
London W1

Bibliography

MILITARY FIGURES

The Collector's Guide to Model Tin Figures, Ortmann, London, 1974
Figurines et Soldats de Plomb, Marcel Baldet, Paris, 1961
Model Soldiers, W Y Carman, London, 1973
Model Soldiers, A Collector's Guide, John Garratt, London, 1971
Model Soldiers, Armies in Miniature, Introduced by Massimo Alberini, London, 1972
Model Soldiers for the Connoisseur, John Garrett, London, 1972
Old British Model Soldiers, 1893–1918, L W Richards, London, 1969
Les Petits Soldats de Strasbourg, Paul Martin, Strasbourg, 1950
Der Zinnsoldat, T Hampe, Berlin, 1924

TOYS

A History of Toys, Antonia Fraser, London, 1966
Antique Toys and Their Background, Gwen White, London, 1971
Toys, Patrick Murray, London, 1968
Toys in America, Inez and Marshall McClintock, Washington DC, 1961

CONSERVATION

Application of Science in the Examination of Works of Art, Museum of Fine Arts Seminar, Boston, 1965
Design for Scientific Conservation of Antiquities, R Organ, London, 1968
The Deterioration and Preservation of Library Materials, Edited by H W Winger and R D Smith, University of Chicago, 1970
Plastics in the Modern World, E G Couzens and V E Yassley, London, 1968
Bulletin of the British Model Soldier Society, London, 1963

Index